I AM
WITH YOU
ALWAYS

I AM WITH YOU ALWAYS

True Stories of
Encounters with Jesus

G. SCOTT SPARROW, ED.D.

BANTAM BOOKS
NEW YORK TORONTO LONDON SYDNEY AUCKLAND

I Am with You Always
A Bantam Book / April 1995

All rights reserved.
Copyright © 1995 by G. Scott Sparrow

Book design by Donna Sinisgalli

Library of Congress Cataloging-in-Publication Data
Sparrow, Gregory Scott.
  I am with you always : true stories of encounters with Jesus /
Gregory Scott Sparrow.
      p.   cm.
  Includes bibliographical references.
  ISBN 0-553-09713-X
  1. Jesus Christ—Apparitions and miracles.   I. Title.
BT580.A1S62   1995
232.9′7—dc20
                                        94-29679
                                        CIP

Published simultaneously in the United States and Canada

Bantam Books are published by Bantam Books, a division of Bantam
Doubleday Dell Publishing Group, Inc. Its trademark, consisting of
the words "Bantam Books" and the portrayal of a rooster, is Registered in
U.S. Patent and Trademark Office and in other countries. Marca Registrada.
Bantam Books, 1540 Broadway, New York, New York 10036.

PRINTED IN THE UNITED STATES OF AMERICA

BVG   0 9 8 7 6 5 4 3 2 1

To Hugh Lynn—

who knew Jesus as a friend

CONTENTS

FOREWORD

BY MORTON KELSEY

It is astounding enough that Jesus appeared to his disciples and friends after his death. But it is even more astounding that he has never ceased appearing. Indeed, from the kind of accounts presented in this book, we can reasonably conclude that Jesus still appears today—healing and transforming people just as he ministered to his brokenhearted and defeated disciples. Once the despairing band of ordinary men and women experienced the risen Jesus, they went forth exhibiting an incredible faith and love that eventually conquered the mighty Roman Empire, which had tried to destroy them. Similarly, when people experience Christ today, they find encouragement, help in the midst of darkness, and sometimes healing of the mind and body. Further, Christ instills the conviction that, ultimately, all will be well—and that the eternal love they have experienced in this world will be theirs in the world to come.

I Am with You Always is the first discerning and comprehensive account of how people still experience Christ today. What is surprising to me is that no one has previously taken the trouble to collect and explain the meaning of these experiences. This fascinating book conveys a wealth of both religious and psychological wisdom.

There has been a recent interest in angels and their appearances to individuals. In response to this growing interest, major newspapers and book publishers have been willing to report experiences of these more-than-human realities with which humans can nonetheless relate and communicate. Within the Christian tradition, however, the risen

Christ is closer to the Divine than even the angelic hosts. If so, then the experiences of the Christ in *I Am with You Always* will likely bring readers even closer to the eternal reality that we can know in this life, and convey a deeper understanding of the nature of everlasting life.

For more than forty years, I have been studying the religious experiences that form the foundation of all the great religions.[1] However, much of Western religion has been influenced and contaminated by an overly materialistic world view. This view states that *only* the physical world is real and that human beings are limited to the information that they receive through the five physical senses.

John Polkinghorne—physicist and theologian and president of Queen's College, Cambridge—reminds us that *both* theology and theoretical physics deal with a world that cannot be experienced directly through the five senses. From this viewpoint, the spiritual world is just as real as the physical one.

But why is contact with the spiritual world so apparently rare? Several thinkers have suggested that our physical experiences are filtered through the reducing valve of the brain and nervous system. The information that comes out of the reducing valve concerns only those data necessary to keep us alive in this physical world.

In the course of my years of study into religious experiences, I have found that the dream is the natural altered state of consciousness through which all of us make nightly contact with that realm of reality that has not been filtered through the reducing valve of the brain and senses. Visions, in contrast, differ from dreams *only because we experience them while we are awake* rather than asleep. In other words, *the content of the dream is the same as that of a vision*, except that in visions we are in touch with two different realms of reality at the same time. Hallucinations can occur whenever we lose the ability to tell the difference between the vision and our waking world.

In meditation, another fertile arena for receiving visionary experiences, we can enter the realm of dreams and visions and can even encounter the Creator. When this happens, the Holy One sometimes appears as ineffable light, and sometimes as the risen Jesus. In other experiences, individuals may perceive an angel, another religious figure, or a formless sense of divine presence. Because of the vast scope of these experiences, the author has quite wisely limited himself to experiences of the risen, or eternal, Christ.

Jesus began appearing to people immediately after his death. After he was crucified by the Romans on the day before Passover in A.D. 29, his terrified disciples hid in fear that they might be sought out and forced to meet their master's fate. On Sunday, Jesus appeared first of all to Mary Magdalene, whose grief was turned into pure joy by the evidence that her beloved Lord was alive. Soon after, Jesus fell into step on the road to Emmaus with two grieving followers and revealed himself to them as he broke the bread they prepared to eat together. When he then vanished, these two awestruck followers of Jesus ran back to Jerusalem to share their incredible good news with the hiding disciples. Then they all saw Jesus standing in their midst in his glorified, transcendent body. Then he disappeared again. Jesus' numerous appearances prepared his friends, family members, and disciples to expect him to make good on his promise to be present with them always.

Twice more Jesus appeared: to Thomas and then to the disciples fishing on the Sea of Galilee. Then came a final parting when Jesus disappeared from their sight in a blaze of glory. This event is particularly significant. They knew that they would not experience him in the same physical-spiritual body again. They had come to understand that he was still just as much present as when they had walked the roads of Galilee together. They knew that he would always be with them, and that they had lost nothing. Instead of sorrow, they returned to Jerusalem with great joy to await the gift of the Holy Spirit. Had modern physicists or astronomers been present, they might have used the words of Howard Chandler Robbins's hymn to describe their experience.

And have the bright immensities received our risen Lord,
Where light years frame the Pleiades and point Orion's sword?

Do flaming suns his footsteps trace through corridors sublime,
The Lord of Interstellar space and Conqueror of time?
The heaven that hides him from our sight knows neither
near nor far;
An altar candle sheds its light as surely as a star,
And where his loving people meet to share the gift divine;
There stands he with unhurrying feet, there heavenly
splendors shine.[2]

For nearly two thousand years people have continued to experience the presence of the risen, cosmic Christ. Some momentous events of world history have occurred because of encounters with this Being. Saul of Tarsus encountered Christ as an orb of blinding light on the road to Damascus. As he was going there to persecute Jesus' followers in that city, Christ spoke to him, and Saul was transformed. Then Christ appeared to Ananias. Against his will, Ananias met with Saul and helped transform him into Paul, the apostle to the Greek world.

For nearly three centuries, Christians were persecuted throughout the Roman Empire. Then Emperor Constantine had a vision of a flaming cross in the sky and heard the words: "In this sign you will conquer."

The emperor could make no sense of the sign until Jesus, carrying this symbol, appeared to Constantine in a dream and explained that it was made of the first two letters of Christ in Greek. Under this sign Constantine defeated the pagan emperors who had been persecuting Christians for nearly three hundred years. One of Constantine's first acts was to abolish the persecution of Christians. It is difficult for us to imagine the momentous impact of his decision upon the Christian fellowship and upon world history.

Hundreds of years later, St. Francis of Assisi was praying before a crucifix and had a vision of Jesus speaking to him. With this inspiration Francis became a model of divine love and revived a dormant and cynical church. Jesus had come again at a crucial moment in the unfoldment of his church.

John Newton was the captain of a slave ship until he dreamed of meeting the Christ, who saved him from disaster. He left his infamous trading, went to the seminary, and became a minister. He wrote many of the greatest Christian hymns, among them "Amazing Grace." His dream of a forgiving Christ was the amazing grace that saved him.

In 1895, one of the leading pastors in the Baptist Church—A. J. Gordon—wrote his spiritual autobiography. In it he describes a powerful dream in which he noticed a stranger in the church, but he forgot to look for him after the service. He asked a man sitting next to the stranger who it was sitting next to him. The gentleman replied: "Why, do you not know that man? It was Jesus of Nazareth." Gordon expressed his dismay at not meeting Jesus. The man replied nonchalantly: "Oh, do not be troubled. He has been here today, and no doubt he will come again." Gordon never preached another sermon without remembering Jesus' words, "Lo, I am with you always." It was the turning point of his ministry.[3]

In his book, *Beyond the Mirror*, Henri Nouwen, a Catholic priest and a widely read writer, has provided a superb description of an experience of the cosmic and personal Christ. At a time when his life hung in the balance, he entered the portals of death and found the risen Jesus there with arms open to embrace him. He also realized that this figure was there for him and at the same time was embracing the whole universe.

This experience was cleansing, healing, and powerful. As he reflected on this experience of Christ's love, Nouwen realized he needed new theological language to convey the depth and breadth of Jesus' all-encompassing caring.[4]

Transforming religious experiences are far more common than we ordinarily realize. In a careful sociological survey, Andrew Greeley discovered that 39 percent of the people surveyed said yes to the question "Have you ever felt as though you were very close to a powerful, spiritual force that seemed to lift you out of yourself?" Greeley discovered that fully half of these people had never told another human being of their experience because they were afraid they would be ridiculed. He also found that religious professionals were the last people with whom this group of people would share their religious experiences.[5]

At an ecumenical conference of some two hundred people, I invited the attendees to write down their most important religious experiences and share them with me. Fully half of the fifty accounts I received described the appearance of Christ—indeed, this was the most significant part of their experience. Thus, these experiences described by Dr. Sparrow need to be taken very seriously, for the healing, loving Christ is nearer than we usually realize.

This truth became evident to me when I learned to listen to my dreams. During a time of inner turmoil and conflict, a Jewish Jungian analyst, who had escaped from a Nazi concentration camp, helped me to see that my dreams were trying to show me the way out of the dead-end street in which I found myself. As I learned the language of dreams and realized I was being led by the Spirit, it then occurred to me that if the Holy One was trying to lead me in my sleep, then this same reality would be available if I consciously turned toward the risen Christ in utter quiet and utter honesty. Eventually, I found that whenever I was in real need and was unable to help myself, I could call out and a light would appear. Out of the light, the cosmic and yet intensely personal Jesus would appear and lead me out of crisis.

One of my most helpful dreams came at a time of real doubt. A part of me doubted that I had a real message to share at the seminary where I was speaking. That night I dreamed of an intense but healing light. In the dream I fell on my knees in awe and wonder. I knew I was in the presence of the Divine.

The light gradually took the form of a human being who walked toward me. I was fearful, but this person took me by the hand, raised me to my feet, and embraced me. I knew it was Christ but I was afraid to ask his name. When I did, he laughingly said: "Hardly Visible." We talked for a while and then he disappeared. I wrote down the dream, went back to sleep, and by morning the darkness and doubt had disappeared. That day, I was able to share the sense of victory—and the deeply felt presence of the risen Christ—with those who were waiting for me to speak.[6]

I AM
WITH YOU
ALWAYS

Introduction

The other day my five-year-old son, Ryan, told my wife and me about a dream he had experienced the night before. He dreamed that he crawled out of bed and headed down the hallway toward our room to get in bed with us. Before he reached our door, however, he saw "this light" reach all the way up to the ceiling. And then he saw a man in the light, a man with a beard whom he knew was Jesus. I asked him how he felt when he saw Jesus. Ryan said, "I was afraid!" When I asked him what else happened, he said that Jesus told him not to be afraid. Then Jesus "vanished" and Ryan awakened.

Why did Ryan dream of Jesus? Perhaps it was because we had read to him about Jesus and the disciples from the time he was an infant. Maybe it was because he eagerly goes to Sunday school every week. Or perhaps it was because I had told him months before something that most of us never consider. I had suggested that he *could* dream of Jesus. And regardless of what one believes about such experiences, one thing is certain: Ryan has come to think of Jesus as someone he can *know*.

In the ensuing chapters, I present a variety of remarkable experiences in which individuals relate how Christ appeared to them in waking visions and nocturnal dreams. Taken together, these experiences raise the possibility that some people will readily accept and others will summarily dismiss—that Christ can be experienced as directly and as personally today as when he walked the earth two thousand years ago.

The reader will enter into the miraculous experience of a terminally ill little girl who was healed by Jesus' touch after her parents had already said their final good-byes, will share the shock of a psychotherapist who turned to see Jesus walking beside her one day, and will feel the incredulous wonder of a woman who reached up and touched Jesus' hair as he knelt beside her and prayed. The reader will feel the shame of the young woman who railed at the unavailability of God only to turn and see Christ smiling warmly at her unbelief, will sense the anxiety of a young man who faced a stern but loving Jesus intent on showing him the mess he'd made, and will feel the relief of a dejected woman who heard Christ say to her, "You always have *me*."

For the purposes of this book, I have defined a Christ encounter as any experience in which a person perceives the presence of a being whom he or she identifies as Jesus or Christ. Admittedly, this definition depends entirely on the witness's impressions during and after the experience. And the definition excludes encounters with other identified or unidentified spiritual beings—valuable experiences that doubtless deserve study, as well. And yet, Jesus Christ occupies a unique and important place in our spiritual, cultural, and psychological lives, regardless of what we profess to believe. As many of the recipients of these experiences have discovered, one does not have to believe any particular thing about Christ in order to find him deeply involved in our most life-changing experiences. Thus, I do not think an apology is in order for restricting this study to experiences that offer a perspective on Christ's apparent intervention in the lives of people today.

The reader may, of course, wonder how I obtained a broad collection of Christ encounter experiences. It was the natural outgrowth of a personal interest in such experiences, which began when I was in college twenty years ago. However, I did not set about to solicit accounts of Christ encounters until after my old friend and college roommate Mark Thurston and I discovered, by chance, that we had both developed a keen interest in researching these experiences. Thereafter, we set about to solicit accounts through several different channels. Many of them were sent to us in the form of letters and audio tapes in response to a magazine article I wrote on the topic of Christ encounters. Other accounts were obtained from audiences at various places in the U.S. and Canada where Mark and I lectured on the topic of Christ encounters and related subjects. A few were also submitted by my counseling clients who either experienced Christ encounters before our therapeutic relationship commenced, or in dreams and visions during the time we worked together.

I spent months reading and rereading the experiences before I was able to discern categorical differences between them. While there is a great deal of overlap among the categories I settled on, I believe that the divisions do represent somewhat distinct categories that are useful for the purposes of analysis and presentation. They are as follows:

- *Awakening* encounters, which are first-time experiences characterized by Christ seeming to introduce himself to the witness. The person, as a rule, is surprised by the encounter and is typically left deeply moved and re-oriented toward life.
- *Physical healing* experiences, in which an ill person receives healing or an alleviation of suffering during a Christ encounter.
- *Emotional healing* encounters, in which the witness experiences relief from depression, fear, and other disabling emotions.
- *Confrontational* encounters, in which the person is confronted with some as-yet unresolved problem that stands in the way of a closer relationship with Christ.
- *Initiation* experiences, in which the witness is confronted with an unresolved problem but is able to respond *during the experience* in a way that resolves the problem. The experience typically culminates in a fuller sense of partnership and communion with Christ.
- *Instructional* encounters, in which Christ issues general or specific instructions regarding the life of the recipient.
- *Confirmational* accounts, in which Christ manifests apparently to praise and reassure the person without regard to any specific problem.

I encountered some difficulty in knowing how to refer to the Being who appears in these experiences. It seems obvious that when we talk about the historic Jesus Christ, we think of Jesus as the man and Christ as his spiritual identity. Furthermore, most Christians—having absorbed the orthodox position on this matter—use the two words together to denote the unique and unprecedented indivisibility of man and God in the incarnation of Jesus. Even if one accepts this traditional doctrine, what are we to make of the contemporary visionary experiences included herein? Is the personal identity of the radiant Being something that "comes with" the experience, or is it imposed by the witness's religious training and cultural programming? Or to put it another way, *Is the person of Jesus an essential and necessary aspect of the radiant Being who manifests in the Christ encounter, or only one of many expressions of a singular Christ Being?*

This question was once considered one of the great mysteries of Christianity. Before an orthodox "solution" emerged several hundred years after Jesus lived, religious authorities and common people alike passionately debated a variety of solutions to this great question. We are supposed to know the answer today; but the question resurfaces anyway, perhaps to remind us that there is a limit to what we can know for sure.

It would be nice if we could look to the Christ encounter itself to resolve this perennial question. But, like the Jesus we encounter in the Gospels, the Being who appears in these accounts seems more interested in *loving and healing* people than in answering age-old questions about his ultimate nature. Perhaps it is because he knows we cannot grasp the truth with our minds, anyway. A famous Eastern teacher once said, "Apply not argument to what is beyond thought." After spending many fruitless hours thinking I could improve on the Master's silence, I now believe that an overly analytical approach to these experiences only gets in the way of knowing the one thing we *can* know—that whatever we call him, and however he may appear to us, he loves us just as Jesus loved his friends.

Given the sensitive and controversial nature of these experiences, I believe the reader should know that I bring to this project something in addition to a researcher's point of view: I bring, as well, the memories of my own Christ encounter experiences.

My first of several such experiences, most of which have been deep dreams, took place in 1975.

I dreamed that I was actually flying around inside a new building with my friend Mark. It seemed we were involved in praying for, or consecrating, the building. At one point, I saw Mark standing in a doorway at the back of the auditorium, talking to someone standing beyond the threshold. I knew it was Jesus! Knowing then that I was dreaming, I anxiously walked toward the door, hoping he would still be there. I passed through the door and looked where I assumed he would be. At first I was only able to see bright white light. But then I could see a man clearly in the midst of the light. He was strikingly handsome.

I stood silent and awed by his presence. I felt great love from him, but sternness, as well. He finally asked me, "Are you ready to leave the earth, yet?" I realized that he was asking if I was ready to die. Startled by the implications of his question, I said, "No." He then said, "Then go out and do what you know to do."

Looking back, I realize that I was wavering at that time in my commitment to the path of service I had chosen. It should come as little surprise that the dream effectively nudged me back on course. His words still remind me to take stock of the work I am doing, and to examine whether it serves him.

Like many of the individuals whose experiences are recounted in the following chapters, I didn't have a conscious personal relationship with Jesus Christ prior to the onset of these experiences. My rather liberal Christian upbringing somehow allowed me to circumvent the whole awkward issue of a personal and ongoing relationship with Christ.

Even after undertaking a daily practice of Christ-centered meditation and prayer during my freshman year in college—which I have continued ever since—the person Jesus did not seem, at that time, very important to me. But once the experiences with Jesus started to happen, I awakened to the fact that he had been, and would continue to be, the central Person in my life.

I realize that my own experience potentially represents both a strength and a weakness as a preparation for writing this book. Fortunately, the literature of religious experience includes a great many works written by individuals who have drawn from their own subjective experiences. One does not have to look very far to find important contributions made by individuals who wrote, at least in part, about their own experiences. In the Christian tradition, Paul remains the most famous, justifying his calling to be the Apostle to the Gentiles on his conversion experience with the risen Christ. And while the early Church fathers almost excluded John's Revelation from the New Testament canon, his vision has become the cornerstone of millennial prophecy. Much later, Jesuit founder St. Ignatius Loyola based his spiritual exercises on experiential methods developed by himself during a long period of convalescence from a war wound.[1]

From a less exclusively Christian orientation, Maurice Bucke's 1901 classic *Cosmic Consciousness*[2] was inspired by his own illumination experience but concentrated primarily on the similar experiences of others. From the Eastern tradition, Gopi Krishna's books have been based almost entirely on his own unsettling but profoundly transformative experiences.[3] And even my own well-received *Lucid Dreaming*[4] is based largely on my own lucid dreams. In this tradition of including one's own experiences as a springboard for addressing what is perhaps a universally available phenomenon, I have included some of my own experiences in this initial presentation of Christ encounters.

Another model that has influenced me in my treatment of Christ encounters is represented by Raymond Moody's ground-breaking work on the near-death experience—*Life After Life*.[5] His work has opened the door for numerous other valuable contributions about near-death experiences, including psychiatrist George Ritchie's *Return from Tomorrow*[6] and Betty Eadie's profoundly moving account of her own near-death experience in *Embraced by the Light*.[7] While Moody did not have a near-death experience of his own to provide the impetus for his pioneering research, his open-minded inquiry has appealed to countless individuals who would otherwise have turned away from such a controversial topic. Moody has set the right tone for those of us who probe respectfully the mysteries of humanity's sacred experiences.

While I remain deeply thankful for the Christ encounter dreams I have had, and sincerely hope to have in the future, they have been, as a rule, sobering reminders of my own periodic neglect of my spiritual calling and the need to resolve longstanding problems. From what I can gather, this is typical for others, too: Christ seems to come to point out—in the most loving way imaginable—where more growth or healing is needed. One woman, whose several accounts are included in the following chapters, believes that Christ more often appears in the dreams and visions of those who are, essentially, "remedial students"— not to those whose faith remains unshaken. Perhaps those who "believe without seeing" derive sufficient sustenance from their faith and have less need of Christ's direct intervention.

I sincerely hope that this book will be seen as a step in the right direction toward providing a forum for sharing experiences that heretofore, for various reasons, have been kept as personal treasures from the world at large.

1

AN OVERVIEW

OF THE CHRIST

ENCOUNTER

PHENOMENON

Laura's doctors were sure that the girl was dying. She, her mother, and her brother had all contracted scarlet fever; but her illness had progressed into spinal meningitis, for which there was no medical treatment at the time. The doctors told her parents they could do nothing, and that she would die an excruciating, screaming death. Her parents were advised not to remain with her to witness her last days. She remembers her parents and the Reverend Lang throwing kisses and waving good-bye to her from the door of her hospital room. Then she remembers "a sea of pain."

Later, after losing her eyesight, she was lying on her right side when she heard a voice behind her say, "Laura, turn over." She said, "No, it hurts too much to move. You come around to this side of the bed." Then the voice said, "I promise you it will not hurt. . . . Turn over." Turning, she saw Jesus. She remembers no other words Jesus said, yet she knows they talked. She watched his hand reach out and touch her thin, twisted leg.

Sometime later, she remembers remarking to a nurse about what pretty red hair she had. The nurse looked at her in surprise, realizing that Laura had greatly improved and had regained her eyesight. She rushed from the room to get the doctors. Soon the room filled up with doctors asking questions. Laura was a very shy person and there were too many doctors, too many questions. But she could talk to the Reverend Lang about what had happened: He was the one person in all the world she wasn't too shy to talk to.

Years later, as an adult, she heard he was preaching nearby and went to see him. His sermon included the story of a little girl who, as she lay dying, had been healed by Jesus.

Laura's experience was an intensely private encounter in the confines of her own blinded state of approaching death. But to the extent that it can still inspire us with the transformative love that she experienced in that moment of healing years ago, it is relevant to us today. Indeed, her account serves to demonstrate how one person's apparent encounter with Christ can continue to inspire hope—if not actual healing—in others who hear or read about it.

Of course it is fair to ask, was Laura's experience what it seemed to be? That is, did Jesus actually heal her? And, more important for the rest of us, does Jesus really manifest himself to individuals today? This might, on the surface, seem like a naive and childish wish. But if one accepts both the possibility of a nonmaterial, or spiritual realm, and the unparalleled spiritual mastery that Jesus exhibited, it requires little stretch of the imagination to answer, Why not? And if we add to this the modern-day testimony of a widening circle of credible witnesses, then we might conclude—with some wonder—that yes, he does.

A LARGELY OVERLOOKED PHENOMENON

Contemporary Christ encounters have thus far received scant attention from theologians and ministers—those who might be expected to recognize their significance. T. R. Morton, author of *Knowing Jesus,* points to the obvious reason the church and its representatives have tended to overlook and discredit such accounts.

> We can well appreciate how the church has always been a bit suspicious of an individual's claim to know Jesus by himself. When you acknowledge the claim, you open the door to all kinds of strange, subjective ideas. You give individual experience precedence over the wisdom of the past. Personal knowledge is always a challenge to accepted opinions and a threat to established institutions. . . . It is no wonder that the church has been chary of these claims.[1]

This attitude is by no means a recent development. Actually, the church's position on such things developed quite early when, in the second century, a man by the name of Montanus claimed to be channeling messages from the risen Christ. Montanus claimed that Christ would soon be returning to erect the New Jerusalem in Montanus's home province in Asia Minor. The church authorities saw this as a self-serving prophecy that would establish a dangerous precedent, and declared it a heresy.[2]

Montanus claimed Christ was speaking *through* him. This conferred upon him an authority that no ordinary person could hope to dispute. But what I've found in my research is that most Christ encounters have Jesus speaking *to individuals about his love for them.* Such interventions seem to inspire spiritual work without conferring political or moral advantage upon the recipient.

Some Christ encounters of this type can be found in the writings of a few contemporary figures who are somewhat outside of mainstream Christianity. For example, Starr Daily, the author of *Love Can Open Prison Doors,* says that his life as a hardened criminal abruptly ended when Jesus came to him in a dream. After a torturous stint in prison, Daily said he saw in a dream "the man whom I'd been trying to hate for years, Jesus the Christ." In the dream, Daily encountered Jesus in a garden.

Jesus approached, his lips moving as though in prayer. He stopped near me eventually and stood looking down. I had never seen such love in human eyes; I had never felt so utterly enveloped in love. I seemed to know consciously that I had seen and felt something that would influence my life throughout all eternity.[3]

It is interesting that Daily had often dreamed as a child of meeting Jesus in the same garden environment but had gradually forgotten the experiences. Significantly, Daily follows a largely forgotten age-old Christian tradition in regarding the dream as an acceptable avenue for directly encountering the Christ. Daily went on from this experience to author numerous books on the healing power of faith in Christ.

Edgar Cayce is another well-known figure who apparently experienced several encounters with Jesus. Known principally for his clairvoyant readings on the holistic treatment of disease, he is probably the most famous and best-documented psychic of the twentieth century.

Cayce was a deeply religious Christian and an immensely popular Presbyterian Sunday school teacher. Yet, he never made his Christ encounters a matter of public record. One of the only ways that we know about his experiences is through a letter he wrote to a friend in 1939.

Often I have felt, seen and heard the Master at hand. Just a few days ago I had an experience which I have not even told the folk here. As you say, they are too scary to tell, and we wonder at ourselves when we attempt to put them into words, whether we are to believe our own ears, or if others feel we are exaggerating or drawing on our imagination; but to us indeed they are often that which we feel if we hadn't experienced we could not have gone on.

This past week I have been quite "out of the running," but Wednesday afternoon when going into my little office or den for the 4:45 meditation, as I knelt by my couch I had the following experience: First a light gradually filled the room with a golden glow, that seemed to be very exhilarating, putting me in a buoyant state. I felt as if I were being given a healing. Then, as I was about to give the credit to members of our own group who meet at this hour for meditation (as I felt each and every one of them were praying for and with me), he came. He stood before me for a few minutes in all the glory that he must have appeared to the three on the Mount. Like yourself, I heard the voice of my Jesus say, "Come unto me and rest."[4]

In addition to his extraordinary faith, Cayce's actual encounters with Jesus probably had something to do with sustaining his commitment to a life of serving others. Considering how little time he took for himself during his later years—when his reputation was attracting a never-ending stream of requests for his psychic readings—one is left to conclude that he derived the greatest satisfaction and meaning in life from serving the Lord, who had appeared to him during his hour of need.

Psychiatrist George Ritchie has reported one of the most detailed Christ encounters in the literature. While his Christ encounter has been thought of as primarily a near-death experience (NDE)—perhaps the most famous NDE on record—it is still, above all, an encounter with Jesus Christ. As we shall see in the following chapters, very little meaningful distinction can be made between near-death Christ encounters and those occurring in non-life-threatening circumstances.

While Ritchie was ill with pneumonia, he was administered a drug to which he reacted so severely that he was considered clinically dead for several minutes prior to his resuscitation. During this interval, Ritchie experienced an encounter with Jesus and, presumably, a detailed escorted view of the afterlife.

As in so many Christ encounters, when Jesus appeared to Ritchie, he realized:

☞

This person was power itself, older than time and yet more modern than anyone I'd ever met.

Above all, with that same mysterious inner certainty, I knew that this man loved me. Far more even than power, what emanated from this Presence was unconditional love. An astonishing love. A love beyond my wildest imagining. This love knew every unlovable thing about me . . . and accepted and loved me just the same.[5]

One might think that such experiences would come to a very few devout individuals. But from what I have discovered in my preliminary research, Christ encounters apparently happen as much to ordinary individuals who are simply striving in their own way to do their best. From a scriptural standpoint, this is what one might expect, for Jesus made it clear to his followers that he would manifest himself to anyone who loved him and followed his commandments: "He that hath my commandments, and keepeth them, he it is that loveth me: and he that loveth me shall be loved of my Father, and I will love him, and manifest to him" (John 14:21). Understandably, most of us give this promise little thought. Or if we do, we disqualify ourselves without examining the reasons. Feeling unworthy, we may assume that Jesus would manifest only to those who live exceedingly virtuous lives, and that rules most of us out. Or, feeling insignificant in the cosmic scheme of things, we assume that he would manifest himself only to individuals who have far greater needs than our own. In this vein, one client of mine, who prayerfully calls upon the assistance of spirit guides and Eastern gurus, told me that Jesus had much more important things to do than to attend to her.

Even if we allowed ourselves to hope for such a visitation on the basis of Jesus' recorded promises, what if he did not come? Would that not underscore our sense of unworthiness or our feelings of abandonment? Or, maybe worse yet, if he did come, what would he require of us? A nurse told me that she dreamed she looked out of the window and saw the bright light of the rising sun and Jesus knocking on the emergency room door. Not wanting to face him, she went up to the window and closed the blinds. I can still see the anguish in her face as she told me about this—her one and only Christ encounter. Another person intentionally sought an encounter with Christ, and thereafter dreamed that a basement door opened in her home and light poured out. She knew Christ was coming up the steps and would appear at any moment. She ran to the door and slammed it.

How many of us are ready for such a meeting? Are we really ready to hear what this Being has to say to us?

THE PROBLEM OF TELLING OTHER PEOPLE

Samuel Johnson once said, "Wonders are willingly told and willingly heard." And yet, it seems that the act of sharing a Christ encounter is strewn with interpersonal difficulties. When one believes himself to have encountered Jesus, an intimidating set of problems arises to legislate against sharing this otherwise wondrous experience with others.

Some may be afraid that the experience will be seen as corny and all too conventional—part of the allegedly outworn paternalistic religion of the past. Others probably worry about being seen as inflated with their own sense of importance. And still others may refrain from disclosing the details of such encounters because they are afraid of being judged crazy or called liars of the worst kind. In many of the letters I've received from persons who believe they have encountered Christ, the letter begins with such words as, "I know you won't believe me, but. . . ."

There is also the problem of stirring up feelings of inadequacy in other people who have not had such experiences. Even if they share a worldview that allows for such encounters, it is by no means a sure thing that they will be secure enough in their own spirituality to hear it with an open mind. Jesus, himself, admonished his followers on several occasions to "tell no man" about what they'd experienced with him; and his statement about not casting one's pearls before swine is well-known.

Even religious authorities may not be able to hear about Christ encounters with an open mind. One woman told us that she finally worked up her nerve to share her Jesus experience with two different priests. The first man listened to what she told him, then resumed talking about altogether unrelated matters, as though he had not even heard her. The second priest became angry, saying that he had sought such an experience all his life. Who was she, he asked, to have been so blessed by Jesus' presence? In recognition of this dilemma, C. S. Lewis wrote, "Once the layman was anxious to hide the fact that he believed so much less than the vicar; he now tends to hide the fact that he believes so much more."[6]

For these and other reasons, it is not surprising that people generally refrain from sharing such experiences. Unfortunately, their silence creates the impression that Christ encounters are less common than they actually are. Because of this, one of the purposes of this book is to provide a vehicle for sharing these experiences so that the recipients can avoid some of the sticky interpersonal problems cited above. By preserving the anonymity of contributors, this book provides a way for them to relate their Christ encounters without having to worry about reactions from others.

On the receiving end, the sympathetic reader is perhaps in a much better position to appreciate the experiences without knowing the other persons, or having them present. By reading multiple accounts of anonymous, ordinary individuals, the reader might more easily resist the inclination to conclude that the other person is a better, more virtuous individual who deserves to have such encounters. And, relieved of the burden of knowing the other person's personal foibles, the reader may also be able to appreciate the validity of the account without letting his knowledge of the other person get in the way. Thus, except for losing whatever benefits might result from a direct person-to-person exchange, a collection of anonymous written accounts can, arguably, assist both witnesses and readers in reaping the greatest benefit from Christ encounters.

HOW CAN WE EVALUATE THE VALIDITY OF CHRIST ENCOUNTERS?

Given the difficulty, if not presumption, in evaluating any intensely meaningful experience, we must be careful not to impose some arbitrary set of beliefs or doctrines—no matter how widely accepted—upon Christ encounters. And yet, most people would probably agree that an important facet of any investigation into Christ encounters should involve some kind of evaluation concerning the degree of relevancy or validity exhibited by a particular experience.

There are precedents that can assist us in this regard, for evaluating the validity of spiritual experiences—especially prophetic pronouncements—is an age-old concern. In the Old Testament, Jeremiah suggests a simple test of validity—that the prophecy come to pass! He suggests that "when the word of the prophet comes to pass, *then* shall the prophet be known, that the Lord has truly sent him" (Jer. 29:9). And Jesus' own words, "By their fruits, ye shall know them," expands Jeremiah's test of prophecy into a general rule for evaluating the quality of our lives as a whole. By making the fruits of our beliefs and experiences—the *good* that comes from them—the *only* criterion by which we are judged, Jesus provided a way for us to avoid what might be called the "demonization" of other peoples' beliefs and experiences.

Of course, people have rarely been content to abide by the test that Jesus espoused. A person's beliefs—and the particular details of their personal spiritual experiences—have traditionally figured much more prominently than the fruits of their lives in determining their treatment from others. Indeed, concern about the validity of spiritual beliefs and experiences reached absurd proportions during the Spanish Inquisition, when even the most devout individuals came under suspicion. The plight of Teresa of Avila (1515–1582) is a good example of how attempts to evaluate spiritual experiences have too often mirrored the fears and biases of the evaluators.

The young and vivacious Carmelite nun envisioned Jesus regularly, sometimes when she would be conversing with the visitors who came to the convent each day. When the local religious authorities, who were threatened by her growing influence, found out about her visions, they called for an investigation that immediately threatened her life. Everyone knew she would be burned if her experiences were judged demonic. Fortunately, the Jesuits intervened to supervise the investigation and to protect her from the Inquisition.

But while her Jesuit protector was temporarily away, Teresa was forced by less sympathetic local church officials to do something totally repugnant to her: She was told to test the vision by making an obscene gesture to the Lord. "Give it the fig!" (a clenched fist with the thumb crossed under the index finger and over the middle finger, signifying a woman's vulva) the inquisitor demanded. "If it is the devil, he may take it as an expression of your contempt, and if it is the Lord, he will not hold it against you, for you are merely obeying an order which I have given you to protect our holy faith."

With great sadness, she complied. "This business of giving the fig," she related, "caused me the greatest sorrow, for my next vision was one of the suffering Lord." Even so, Christ knew her heart, and he did not abandon her for her compliance.[7]

Eventually, even the considerable authority of the Inquisition could not discredit Teresa. One of the most notorious inquisitors finally acknowledged the authenticity of her visions. She went on to reestablish the Carmelite order as a beacon of spirituality during a relatively corrupt and materialistic era.

Given the presumption involved in trying to validate a Christ encounter, I have made little attempt to conduct this evaluation for the reader, except to point out when a Christ encounter contains possibly controversial or unorthodox content.

HOW DO WE KNOW IF CHRIST ENCOUNTERS ARE "REAL"?

It is easy to dismiss a Christ encounter—particularly one that happens in a dream—as a purely subjective experience, for these experiences generally fall outside the range of ordinary waking experiences that are composed, in large part, of external events that can be verified by others. But if one is so inclined, much of our experience in life can be similarly undermined: One can dismiss virtually any private experience, including the mere act of thinking, because there is no way to confirm the independent existence of anything unless it can be viewed by others. And yet, whoever takes this position is eventually faced with the absurdity of it. After all, what scientist has yet seen a black hole or a quark? We forget that science, too, operates on faith and conjecture when it comes to the most profound mysteries of the universe.

Of course we would all like to have proof to substantiate the reality of our most precious experiences. But *our ability to prove our experiences diminishes as we approach that which potentially holds the greatest meaning for us.* How can we prove love, faith, or wisdom? Ultimately, perhaps, we are left with only the irrefutable conviction of those who have had certain experiences, and the deeply resonating affirmative response of many of those who still have not. Others are free to criticize such claims, but a careful analysis of much of what passes as objective criticism often reveals a defense of simply another form of faith in what cannot be proven. Author Henry Fielding essentially proclaimed the absurdity of most criticism when he asserted, " 'Til they [his own critics] produce the authorities by which they are designated judges, I shall not plead their jurisdiction."[8]

In spite of the unprovability of something as potentially meaningful as Christ encounters, one can at least confirm the psychological "reality" of something invisible by establishing that the experience is widespread and has predictable, recurrent qualities. Certainly, we now agree that everyone dreams, even though we accept the fact that we cannot produce them for scrutiny. Even much less common subjective experiences can, in time, become a widely accepted "reality" if enough witnesses come forward with similar accounts. For instance, Raymond Moody, George Ritchie, Betty Eadie, and others have provided compelling evidence of the universality of the near-death experience—to the point where many people believe that what persons experience on the verge of death points to the certainty of an afterlife. In a similar way, this book may contribute to the acceptance of the Christ encounter as a universally occurring phenomenon with predictable features, and promote further inquiry into the subject.

HOW CHRIST ENCOUNTERS COME TO US

The Christ encounters in the following chapters occurred in a variety of states of mind. Almost half of the experiences were waking visions. A few occurred when it was unclear whether the person was awake or asleep. In these, the witnesses have typically been lying in bed during the encounter.

Over half of the experiences collected were unusually deep and clear dreams. In most of these, the witnesses were not aware at the time that they were dreaming. A few, however, were "lucid dreams," in which the dreamer realizes *consciously* that he is in a dream. Similar to "out-of-body" experiences, the lucid dreamer enters the dream as a fully aware, interacting participant while the body remains apparently fast "asleep." In an out-of-body experience, the person also seems to be outside of his physical body during the experience, and often observes his sleeping body from an external vantage point.

Only one of the accounts was clearly a near-death experience (that of K.V.D. in chapter 2). However, several accounts—most of which were deep dreams—closely resembled NDEs, except that none of them occurred in life-threatening circumstances.

I believe it is important to examine some of our assumptions and biases regarding the states of mind in which these Christ encounters have occurred. Otherwise, we might unfairly overvalue *or* undervalue an experience merely because of the state of mind in which it took place.

Dreams. It is probably true that most of us give waking visions more credence than dreams. We are somehow reassured when a person tells us he was on his feet with his eyes open when it all happened.

But dreams have not always been considered less real or meaningful than waking experiences or so-called waking visions. Morton Kelsey's analysis of both the Old and New Testaments reveals that dreams and visions, or rather the singular concept of the dream-vision, occupies a central place in the Judeo-Christian tradition. Actually,

Kelsey points out that the ancient position was to regard the dream as *the state in which a vision naturally occurred*. The vision, according to this view, is the content of the dream. Although the vision can intrude upon waking awareness, the dream was considered the natural state in which visions were experienced.[9]

Kelsey is fond of displaying a Bible from which all references to dreams and visions have been removed: There is simply not much left. While it is sometimes unclear in the biblical narrative whether the writers were referring to waking visions or dream-visions, since they were regarded as synonymous, we find many unambiguous references to dreams. Certainly Joseph's dream of the angel warning him to flee Herod's soldiers can be seen to be sufficient evidence that dreams can communicate God's will. And Peter's dream, which prompted him to accept an invitation to dine at the "unclean" table of a non-Jew, signified the beginning of a new attitude toward Gentile followers of Christ.

Kelsey also points out that during the first few centuries of the Christian era, the great spokesmen of the Church typically regarded the dream very highly. Origen asserted that the dream-vision was an important part of God's method of revealing himself to individuals. He divided them into two categories: direct and symbolic experiences. He reported that many of the early Christians were actually converted to the new faith through dreams and visions. For instance, Gregory Thaumaturgus, a major force in the early Church, was converted from his pagan beliefs in a dream of John the Beloved and Mary, the mother of the Lord.

Another early Church father, Cyprian, claimed to have experienced direct manifestations of God in his dreams. He even had one dream in which a young man of striking appearance informed him of his imminent martyrdom. And Constantine's famous dream of Christ on the eve of his great military victory not only accounted for his conversion, but also made a place for Christianity in the Roman empire—thus ensuring the religion's survival through a torturous time.

Like Origen, many of the early Church fathers believed that dreams originated from different levels of the soul. This approach allowed for the confusing and disturbing nature of many dreams without ruling out the possibility of God speaking through other, clearer dreams. This sophisticated multileveled view of dreams was gradually forgotten as the Church adopted the more arid, rational theology of Thomas Aquinas. Fortunately, this earlier understanding has been resurrected in the modern work of psychiatrist Carl Jung, who reasserted a multilevel view of dreams. Even as an empirical scientist, Jung was compelled to admit that the Divine spoke to us through dreams emanating from the deeper levels of the psyche.

Even so, the belief that dreams are inferior to waking experiences still prevails. To give dreams a fresh chance, we might do well to look at *the extent to which the dream involves the person in a dynamic and rich interaction with Christ and with the thrust of his message.* By looking at it this way, the dream-based Christ encounter may emerge as an experience on an equal footing with waking encounters. Indeed, we might even conclude that the capacity of dreams to symbolize complex truths may better serve the purposes of the Christ encounter in many instances.

Lucid Dreams and Out-of-Body Experiences.   A few of the Christ encounters occurred when the witnesses were fully conscious and aware of what was taking place but were nonetheless in a dream or a nonphysical realm. The presence of full waking awareness goes a long way toward satisfying our ordinary concept of what is "real." But since these experiences took place while the witnesses were ostensibly "out" of touch with their bodies, they remain nonphysical experiences—like ordinary dreams. Paul himself alluded to this feature of his conversion experience when he said, "Whether in the body, I cannot tell; whether out of the body, I cannot tell: God knoweth." (2 Cor. 12:2)

Those who have had such nonphysical experiences report, paradoxically, that the vividness and sense of reality *exceeds* our everyday sensory experience. These experiences owe their "realness" to their amazing clarity and intensity, not to their physicality. Ordinary dreams in general—and lucid dreams and out-of-body experiences in particular—challenge us to consider why we cling so tightly to the idea that an experience in the physical world is inherently more meaningful and valuable than a nonphysical experience. This requirement would disqualify many of the most moving, life-transforming experiences included in this volume. Actually, if we examine each experience closely, we find that virtually all of the experiences included herein took place outside the realm of normal sensory channels. Just because the individual remained aware of his surroundings does not mean that the vision was any more physical than a nocturnal dream. Such experiences may say more about the capacity of the mind to operate on more than one level at a time than about the *physical reality* of what the individual observes.

Near-Death Experiences.   As already mentioned, one of the Christ encounters also satisfies the definition of a near-death experience (NDE). A few other experiences, which did not take place under life-threatening circumstances, exhibit many of the features of an NDE, such as a life review, an encounter with Christ, and the message that the time is not yet right for the person to remain in the afterlife.

Actually, NDEs in which Christ appears can be considered a *category* of the Christ encounter phenomenon. After all, Christ encounters occur in a variety of altered states of consciousness, as well as in (or overlapping with) ordinary waking consciousness. They are not exclusively associated with physical trauma or any other single mental or physical condition. So the additional designation as an NDE, a dream, or an out-of-body experience should not distract us from the focus of this work. For the purposes of this study, the particular *state of consciousness* in which the Christ encounter occurs should remain secondary to the larger question of whether the *content* of the experience satisfies the definition of a Christ encounter—an experience in which one perceives the presence of Christ.

What do these various states of mind have in common? Perhaps they all assist the individual in surrendering a limited ego- and body-based identity. Whether this surrender occurs involuntarily—as during physical or emotional crises—or through the intentional spiritual practices of prayer and meditation, it seems as though the Christ encounter witnesses all report arriving at a state of openness and surrender prior to the manifestation of the Christ. In the Revelation, Jesus said to John, "I stand at the door and knock," implying that Christ is always waiting for us to do our part. And what is that? It may be that all of our efforts to bring Christ into our lives end—and finally succeed—in simply surrendering to a relationship with him.

HOW CHRIST ENCOUNTERS FIT INTO MODERN CHRISTIANITY

Since I am not a theologian, I am not prepared to assess thoroughly the Christ encounter's place in Christian tradition and theology. However, it occurs to me that there are two traditional ways of analyzing the Christ encounter from within the Christian tradition: as a precursor to the Second Coming and/or as an indication of the availability of the risen Christ to people today. The first might be called the millennial approach and the second, the perennial approach.

The Millennial Approach.   As we approach the end of the twentieth century and the second millennium, there is a resurgence of interest in various prophecies that allegedly pertain to these times. A great many Christians—in particular, fundamentalist Christians—expect the eventual return of Jesus Christ. There are numerous versions of how this might take place, but the more orthodox view is based on the expectation of an eventual bodily return of Jesus Christ.

The widespread belief in Christ's Second Coming originally grew out of the Old Testament messianic prophecies that foretold of a savior who would come in power and glory to establish God's kingdom on earth. Because Jesus was crucified before he could fulfill these expectations, his Jewish followers came to believe that his Second Coming was imminent. Jesus' own words support this view in some of the New Testament passages, most specifically when he promised to return and fulfill the messianic prophecies before his own generation had passed away (Matt. 24:35).

When this did not happen, many of his followers struggled to reconcile the apparent discrepancies between the Old Testament prophecies of a powerful messiah and Jesus' death as a criminal. Those who anticipated the fulfillment of these prophecies faced more and more of a problem as time passed accounting for why Jesus had not returned. They had a choice. They could look to the future for his return, or they could accept Jesus' role as redeemer through his sacrifice and resurrection.

The Perennial Approach.   Jesus began appearing to his followers within days of his crucifixion. They did not always recognize him at first, but there was no doubt that he had appeared to them. No one came to regard this as the Second Coming, because it still didn't fit the prophecies of a messiah who would come in power and glory. He appeared to them ostensibly to show them that he was indeed alive and would continue to be available to those who loved him—not to set up a kingdom among men. He also told them that he hadn't yet ascended. So, it was a special transitional period during which Christ walked among men in his resurrected body.

But following Christ's ascension, something altogether unprecedented occurred: Paul encountered the risen Christ—not as an embodied man but as a formless, radiant Being who identified itself as Jesus. Thereafter, Paul began to offer a perspective that complemented the traditional emphasis on the Second Coming as the fulfillment of Jesus' work. He certainly embraced the traditional prophecies about Christ's return; in his later writings, however, he shifted to more of an emphasis on the resurrection as the wholly sufficient fulfillment of

Jesus' mission to us. Recognizing the problem of basing one's faith on an event that might not happen for a very long time, Paul shifted early Christians away from waiting for Jesus to return and refocused them on the ever-present redemptive power of Christ's resurrection, exemplified by his own dramatic conversion. He thus freed Christianity from a deadline, and opened up a future in which Christ's undiluted spiritual influence could be palpably felt by each and every one of us.

As the reader shall see, the Christ encounters in the ensuing chapters tend to support the perennial view of the risen Christ's intercessory role in our lives. However, not one of the experiences recounted in these pages refutes the possibility of a Second Coming.

THE POSITIVE EFFECT OF SHARING CHRIST ENCOUNTERS

Not all Christ encounters are equally dramatic and uplifting. And yet, they almost always seem to represent a pivotal moment in a person's life in which encouragement or healing seems desperately needed, or in which Christ calls the individual to serve him in some way. Of course, it is not always clear what specific need the encounter has served, or exactly what has taken place.

Some Christ encounters are so moving that when they are told, they awaken in the listener a profound sense of love, self-acceptance, and forgiveness. These experiences seem to speak to a depth in the human psyche that transcends religious and interpersonal differences. If so, we owe it to ourselves to consider the sharing of these accounts as a form of therapeutic experience. Further, there is evidence to suggest that sharing Christ encounters can open up the listener to having his or her own encounter.

When this book was still in the early stages, I was working with a young man who had derived a great deal of strength from his relationship with Christ. As we confronted his rather intractable drug addiction problem, we would often talk about Jesus' love for his unruly disciples and his forgiveness for their weaknesses.

During our work together, I often had occasion to share some of the Christ encounters I'd been collecting for the book. One day, when he was feeling particularly despondent, we again began talking about people who had experienced Christ's intervention in their lives, including Bill Wilson, the founder of Alcoholics Anonymous. My client expressed a hope that he, too, might be blessed with spiritual healing, since all other remedies had failed. Specifically, he hoped that Jesus would come to him to help him end his long-standing problem. He had always been able to relate to Jesus as a person and had even written some moving poetry and prose about him; but he had never experienced a direct encounter with Christ.

As he talked on about his desire for such an intervention, I thought about a woman who had experienced Jesus actually coming to her bedside while she prayed one night (M.L.P.#1 in chapter 2). In that experience, she had reached up and felt his hair, confirming that he was, indeed, present in a very physical way. As I imagined that experience happening to her, I began hoping that the man's yearnings might be answered in a similar fashion. I am sure that my own inability to help my client overcome his problem fueled my hopes.

Suddenly, I felt "struck" by what felt like a wave of energy coming from my left. It felt oddly familiar. I knew from my own earlier Christ encounters that this feeling preceded the coming of white light or Jesus himself. I continued to sit in silence, looking at and listening to my client as usual, not knowing where this was going to go. After a few moments, my client stopped talking in midsentence, looked in the direction from which I had felt the wave of energy come, and then asked something like, "What's happening? Something's happening here." Then a second wave hit and I felt almost overwhelmed by it—as if I were becoming very small and surrounded by someone dwarfing me with power and love. I was afraid and simultaneously frustrated by this fear. I suggested that we close our eyes and be still. As we did, I saw white light well up in my visual field. The sense of presence lasted for several minutes. Later on when we talked about the incident, we discovered that we had both felt a palpable sense of Christ's presence with us.

As far as I can see, there was no instantaneous healing for my client. But the event fortified the man in his commitment to overcome his problem. And his movement toward that end is clearly evident at the time of this writing. For myself, it served to convince me that the Christ encounter could be an imminent possibility in my counseling work as well as in the more familiar, private confines of my deep meditations and dreams—especially if both parties share an interest and willingness to discuss such experiences as a way to encourage his coming.

Many of us would doubtless be disappointed if we set about to experience a Christ encounter. For reasons unknown to us at the present time, such experiences are still apparently hard to come by. Consequently, we should perhaps be willing to derive whatever meaning we can from the experiences of others, rather than to make such experiences a criterion of spiritual attainment or the basis of our self-worth. There is ample precedent for this approach. The history of Christianity reveals a willingness among Christians to study and derive sustenance from the experiences of others, rather than feeling disenfranchised in the face of the apparent good fortune of others. Indeed, the whole historic foundation of Christianity is based on Jesus' encounters with a relatively small group of followers and critics. Modern Christians derive their knowledge of Christ to a large extent from his recorded encounters with other people thousands of years ago. Each parable, each individual gesture of love, and each healing combine to form a cohesive testament to what he was and still is to all people, even though he had direct contact with only a few.

Similarly, if we can accept the stories of the persons whose experiences with Christ are recounted in the following pages, we have an opportunity to derive hope from what is apparently happening in the lives of at least some individuals today. The mere fact that these momentous encounters occur at all might go a long way to deepen our commitment to living according to higher ideals, if not to enhance our readiness to have such an encounter ourselves.

2

The Awakening

Encounter

Few of us, regardless of our religious beliefs, expect to meet Christ face-to-face during our lifetimes. For various reasons, we assume that such things just do not happen to ordinary people. So it should come as no surprise to us that a person's first encounter with Christ usually comes as *quite* a surprise. In these initial encounters, which I have called awakening Christ encounters, Christ's manifestation seems to revolve around the singular aim of awakening the witness to his presence. Typically, the individuals who contributed awakening encounters were involved in spiritual study or seeking at the time but were nonetheless startled when Christ himself appeared.

As one might expect, the impact of this manifestation is considerable: It establishes Christ as a living, caring Being who communicates directly with individuals. Consequently, the experience often signals the beginning of a new phase in one's life, characterized by a commitment to an ongoing one-on-one relationship with Jesus.

The following experience was submitted by a woman who had reservations at first about whether she should share her Christ encounters with readers of this book. In particular, she expressed concern that such accounts might awaken jealousy or a sense of inadequacy in people who have not experienced Jesus in such a direct manner. Believing strongly that her own experiences came to fill a need at the time, she wished to avoid implying that Jesus comes to those who somehow deserve it. Even so, she eventually decided that the potential benefits of sharing her experiences with others outweighed the possible drawbacks.

⁓

My first experience was at night. I had been lying in bed praying. I was pulled away from praying by a light in the hallway outside my room. The light seemed to be coming from down the hall, outside my view. As I watched, the light grew brighter. It seemed to be coming down the hall toward my room.

Then I saw Jesus carrying a candelabra with seven lit candles. He was tall and dressed in a dark blue/purple robe that had crescent moons and stars on it. The edge of the garment and sleeves were trimmed in gold.

He walked into my room, placed the candelabra on the floor, and knelt to pray by the side of my bed.

I moved my right hand and touched his hair.

I shall never forget the way his hair felt. I was engulfed with his love and the soft glow he and the candles brought to the room.

After a while, he picked up the candelabra and walked toward the door. As he walked out of the doorway, I asked, "How can I reach you again?"

He turned and smiled. A warm, radiant smile that had an amused turn to it. His eyes danced playfully, lovingly.

"I'm in the phone book," he replied.

He turned and walked away while I found myself wondering how he would be listed in the phone book. How would I find him? And then I knew that he would be listed under "Emmanuel." When I looked up *Emmanuel* in the dictionary the next day, I discovered that *Emmanuel* means "God is present in the world." (M.L.P.#1)*

An interviewer once asked Carl Jung toward the end of his life if he *believed* in God. After a long pause, he answered, "I don't believe. I know. I know."[1] Whether experience can or should ever fully take the place of faith, M.L.P. can say with a greater degree of certitude than ever before, I *know*.

    M.L.P.'s hesitancy to share her experiences is by no means unusual. Many of the individuals who submitted their accounts said that they had related their experiences to only one or two persons. The Christ encounter leaves a person feeling willing to remain silent, in many instances, to protect the sacredness of the experience. The woman who submitted the following extraordinary encounter did so after years of remaining silent.

I was attending prayer vigil before evening daily Mass. When I got out of my car in the parking lot of Most Holy Trinity Church, I glanced at the clock and knew that the vigil would begin in a few minutes. Hurriedly I approached the street corner and crosswalk. Stopping to look both ways, I was aware of a sudden dark deadness. I looked up over my left shoulder to see very large clouds forming. The wind blew

---

* Each account is identified by the witness's initials. If a witness is quoted more than once, I have added a number after the initials to indicate which account is being presented. To distinguish between witnesses who have the same initials, I have placed an ordinal before the initials. For example, "1st R.P.#2" signifies the second account by a person whose initials are the same as those of at least one other witness.

strongly and I felt a storm approaching. I stopped to watch the quick buildup of clouds overtaking the eastern sky.

From behind the greatest dark cloud, which now appeared to me as a thunderhead, emerged the brightest light I've ever experienced. It filled the remainder of the sky and all about me. I felt short of breath. I could not move. I didn't want to miss this!

From out of this light and on top of the stationary "thunderhead" flowed liquid gold, as though it were being poured. It built up and accumulated in height, from which the form of Jesus appeared.

(Words here seem inadequate to describe the experience. I still cry as I recall the whole experience again.)

I stood in awe and obedience before him. His robe was hooded and fell in soft folds about him. His facial features were not really distinct but were there vaguely. The bright light and gold engulfed me, also. I stared and waited.

From under his robe, the gold poured out forward and fell toward me and the parking lot, much like lava, slowly curving here and then there. As I watched, mentally I told myself that the Lord has come for me. "I am ready," I uttered softly. I felt such joy, such happiness, such excitement, yet my physical body remained very still. The golden path now was almost to the parking lot and about six to ten feet from where I stood. I left my body to meet the path. As I did, the gold stopped flowing. I heard the message, "Not now, listen." I stopped and listened intently, suspended.

"Be in communion with me." I could hear and feel his words. They filled every space within me and about me. Still outside myself and full, I watched as the gold "lava" went back upward to him and all form disappeared. I was back in my body before the Light was gone.

Now my body shook all over. I couldn't settle it down or make it still. I felt confused, and I didn't know if I should go to my car or to prayers. I wanted to shout and jump and dance and cry and laugh with joy all at the same time.

When I entered the church, prayers were in process. I sat where I usually did, next to Sister Mary Damian, one of the leaders of our Tuesday prayer group. I shook noticeably, fumbling in my prayer book to find the correct prayer. I dropped to my knees in frustration and gratitude. Damian, as we call her, helped me by sharing her book with me. I was never able to "get it together" before the service ended.

When I shared a piece of my experience with her, Damian said simply, "I know. It is so beautiful." I felt so full, full of love. Other than Sister Damian, I did not tell anyone about my experience for eight years, and then I shared it with my very close, spiritual friend. I felt that it was such a sacred experience that to tell it as I experienced it might lessen its value.

One thing was *most* clear. I needed to be in communion with our Lord and God. Increasingly I walked a narrower path, with a knowing which surmounted logical reasoning. Trust increased. Discernment became clearer. Barriers melted. Surprises came. Meditation became more frequent. And I realized that being in communion with him means manifesting his love in fuller ways with others, as well as with myself, than I'd known before.

I pray for that direction and listen for his love in whatever way it may come. And then, I await to know how best to pass that Love on to others. It is a knowing, not a message in words. My attentiveness leads me in several directions.

It is time for me to share this experience. (1st M.M.)

Certainly, M.M.'s experience is one of the more dramatic Christ encounters included in this book. One can sense how her devotion had established an opening through which Christ could reach out to her. And one can feel the tremendous love and authority emanating from Christ as M.M. shows herself willing to surrender to him. While her encounter fits the criteria of an awakening encounter, it also includes instruction of a global nature. His admonition to her—to be in communion with him—leaves so much open-ended. Essentially, he implies, Do whatever you must do to be in communion with me. While the *goal* is set by him, the *methods* are up to her. One might say that this captures the essence of Jesus' message, whether one looks at his words in the Gospel record or at contemporary Christ encounters. Even though he wants a person's full commitment, he leaves it up to each person to decide how to accomplish this singular aim.

Indeed, the awakening encounter, in particular, seems to leave a great deal unanswered. Jesus appears briefly and powerfully and then leaves the witness to contemplate the meaning of the experience thereafter. Such is the case with the following account of an eighty-year-old Presbyterian woman who at the age of eighteen experienced her first encounter with Christ in a dream that seemed more real to her than an ordinary dream.

☞

I was 18 years old and vacationing at Ocean View, Virginia, with friends in the month of August.

That night I was sleeping with another girl who was with our party. I went to sleep and during the night I found myself in a huge hall. It was a very beautiful one with beautiful floors and a few white columns. There were hundreds of people there, and Jesus stood at the back of the hall. All the people were on their knees on the floor with their arms outstretched and bowing to him.

I was standing at the back of the hall. When he saw me he made his way slowly through the crowd being careful not to step on anyone. He came to where I was standing and stood in front of me. The light and vibration from his presence was so tremendous that I could hardly bear it in a physical sense. He looked into my eyes, then pointed his forefinger at me and said, "You." His facial expression was stern and yet very loving. His eyes were rather a steel blue. They were clear and I would say more of a blue than a gray. He looked at me with a rather stern expression and at the same time there was great love and tenderness there. His countenance expressed tremendous strength of character and personality, and great love.

I returned to my bed and it was still night. I experienced great fear and tried to lie closer to my friend for comfort. She did not help me at all and I was alone. I went back to sleep. The next morning I felt great joy and happiness, such as I had never experienced in my 18 years. All day I was radiant.

I have not made my story a public thing, as I felt it was too private and special. I have only told it to about four or five people. (M.M.W.)

M.M.W. experienced strong conflicting feelings on the heels of her Christ encounter. There was a lot to be thankful for, but a great deal was left unanswered. Why was he so stern? Why did he come to her? Like many of the encounters with Christ included in this book, this experience was both uplifting and unsettling at the same time. To be completely loved is, perhaps, the ultimate experience. But to be totally known can be painful, especially when our eyes are opened to a forgotten past mirrored in the Knower's eyes. When Christ pointed at M.M.W., she grasped both truths at once. But once she fully experienced her fear, joy prevailed. This indicates again that the overall impact of the Christ encounter is an empowerment and uplifting of the individual, in spite of the painful awarenesses that necessarily accompany the process.

A 41-year-old woman feels that she was called by Christ in her first encounter to involve herself in some form of spiritual work. Two years after her initial Christ encounter, she is still trying to define the deep sense of calling that was stirred to life by Christ's appearance.

~

I was in my bedroom preparing to go to bed when suddenly I saw a man in the doorway. He was dressed in white biblical-type robes and was surrounded by a golden glow. Even the folds of his robes seemed to reflect this golden light. He did not look like the pictures of Jesus that I've seen so often in churches. I've since decided that this was because I've never been satisfied that this is what Jesus must look like. Instead he had shoulder-length dark hair and a beard. I could not clearly see his eyes, yet felt that they reflected a gentle nature. Not a word was spoken. When I first saw him, I was shocked. I told myself my eyes were playing tricks on me, so I closed them tightly and then opened them. He was still there. Again, I closed my eyes and again he was still there. Suddenly, he was gone.

I thought for sure I was going crazy so I made an appointment to talk to a psychologist. I did not tell her what happened, just that there were some problems in my family and I wanted to be sure that I had not inherited any predispositions. She said I tested out fine, although I was showing some signs of stress. (J.F.)

J.F. was left feeling that she had been called by Jesus. But to do what? Months after this first encounter, she dreamed of Jesus again: She saw him and a nun standing nearby, waiting for her. Again, she was left with no clear direction. It is interesting that so many recipients of Christ encounters are left wondering what to do next. One might conclude that the Christ encounter is, as yet, unfinished—that additional installments will eventually complete the picture. It might be hard to believe that Jesus would manifest to us only to leave us with more unanswered questions than before. But perhaps that is one purpose of the Christ encounter—to stir the individual to greater life and to activate an impassioned search for meaning. After all, if Jesus provided all the answers, the newly awakened soul might quickly submit again to slumber.

An 18-year-old woman experienced Jesus coming to her as she dreamed of drowning in her own baptismal waters. Like most awakening accounts, it is enigmatic and powerful, and raises many questions.

About the time of my eighteenth birthday I dreamed one night that I was in a moonlit garden, and three angels appeared to me and asked if I wanted to be baptized. I was awestruck, to say the least, and a bit frightened so I said, "Yes," even though I wasn't sure I did. They led me to a very deep pool. I immediately became very scared because I didn't know how to swim, so I protested that I couldn't get into that pool because I might drown. They assured me that they would watch me and insisted that I go on in. I did and immediately the water started whirling like a whirlpool, faster and faster. I was struggling with all my might to stay up but I kept getting sucked down. I looked up at the angels and they just leaned over the edge, expressionless. They watched me but made no move to help. The pool then seemed like a large deep well. Finally, I was so exhausted, I resigned myself to the idea that I was going to drown.

I looked up one last time and saw Jesus, dressed in a white robe. He reached down and extended his right hand and I reached up with my right hand. I was immediately out of the pool and sitting beside him. I don't remember what he said to me.

I walked around in a kind of glow for weeks but never told anyone about the experience. Finally, I suppressed it and forgot about it until years later. I've since told it several times when I've thought it was appropriate. (1st P.B.)

An interesting aspect of P.B.'s experience is the contrast between the angels, who remain dispassionate throughout, and Jesus, who reaches out to save her. This experience raises questions, not so much about the ultimate nature of angels—which one can never know—but how people understand and experience angels in contrast to Jesus. P.B. perceived them as being unfeeling and unavailable to her in her time of need. Why? It could be because P.B. believed that angels, by virtue of having never been incarnate, could lack a certain empathy that comes from experiencing life as a human being. Jesus lived and died as a man, and thus can presumably understand and empathize with P.B.'s struggles. If, on some level, many of us perceive angels as deficient in the qualities that are so essentially human, why then do so many of us turn to them? It could be that a certain trade-off is involved in whomever we choose as an intermediary between ourselves and God. Because angels remain forever unsullied by life, they can be rather appealing when we feel lost in the human condition. But they lack a certain warmth by virtue of their otherworldliness. Jesus, on the other hand, experienced the joys and hardships of incarnational life; but he has been so explained and analyzed by two thousand years of religion that it is often hard to see the real man behind all of the dogma.

The following dream occurred while the witness was enrolled in a Bible study course on the Book of Daniel. In her dream, the woman experiences Jesus in the midst of radiant white light, a phenomenon often associated with Christ encounters. The experience is both dramatic and unforgettable, as well as simple and unembellished.

⌒

I dreamed I was standing atop a mountain. I looked skyward and saw a bright golden light. As I stared at it, it turned into the most brilliant white light I have ever seen. In the center of the light I saw the face of Christ appear. After gazing at his face I saw what looked like comets shooting this way and that. One landed close to where I was standing and burst into flames.

I awoke and it felt like I was coming out of anesthesia. There is no question in my mind whether or not it was Jesus. You just know. He is the guiding and/or controlling force in my life. (M.D.)

There is an economy of detail in this experience. Jesus does not speak one word, and the encounter seems to take place within the span of a few moments. In spite of its brevity, M.D. was deeply affected by its perceptual vividness and emotional intensity. Like other awakening Christ encounters, this account suggests that they may occur not so much to offer answers or solutions but to *bring into one's awareness* a conscious covenant or a partnership with God.

The experience serves to strengthen M.D.'s conviction that Jesus, himself, is an essential part of her spiritual life. Having seen his face, she makes this obvious conclusion for herself. Yet, it's clearly up to each of us, based on our own experiences, to make our own conclusions regarding the importance of this spiritual being, or any other, in our lives. One Jewish woman I know had her own version of a "Christ" encounter in a very vivid dream. She saw the back of a radiant being who then slowly turned toward her. As the being's face came into view, she saw that the being was a luminous form of herself, reflecting back to her the most exquisite love and acceptance. She, too, encountered a personal embodiment of God; but it was probably different than what most Christians might typically experience. And for some people, having not experienced such a personal manifestation of *any* kind, Jesus or Buddha or even a luminous embodiment of oneself might not adequately convey a more general or universal feeling about God in their lives. One can see that the Christ encounter raises the questions, "How personal does God have to be in my life, and how essential is any one personal expression of God?"

If we knew more about each witness, we would probably conclude that most awakening Christ encounters are healing experiences, as well, which address a particular dimension of the individual's unresolved past. The following account comes across as a classic awakening encounter. It does not directly address a problem in need of healing. However, when questioned further, the individual was able to see that the content of the experience was tailor-made to heal the effects of her emotional abuse as a child.

My experience happened in the sixties during a period of time in which I was seeking.

At the time, I was visiting Yellowstone [National Park]. I had a dream that I was in my own apartment and there was a knock at the door. I opened the door and Jesus stood there. It was all light. He opened his garment and showed me his heart, which was a bright light. He motioned for me to come closer and I saw there were two hearts— joined hearts, interlocking. I'm usually shy and very reserved, but I did not feel that way during the experience. When I woke up I felt wonderful. I found that he really existed. (R.J.#1)

When R.J. was asked about her association to the two hearts, she said, "I think it related to love. I was an unwanted and abused child and had never experienced love. I had to learn love. I believe that one of the hearts was his and one mine." She went on to say that she believed the experience meant for her "to become one with him and love every-body. It's been over twenty years and I remember every detail of that dream."

In many of the Christ encounters included in these chapters, the appearance of brilliant light serves as a prelude to Jesus' personal manifestation. If any experience can be considered the core mystical experience, the experience of brilliant white light is the obvious candidate. Both Christian and non-Christian mystics have observed that the highest spiritual states generally include the interior ex-perience of white or golden light. This phenomenon may occur during meditation, deep prayer, waking visions, or profoundly deep dreams. In support of the centrality of the white light experience, Jung said:

The phenomenon itself, that is, the vision of light, is an experience common to many mystics, and one that is undoubtedly of the greatest significance, because in all times and places it appears as the unconditional thing, which unites in itself the greatest energy and the profoundest meaning.[2]

In Raymond Moody's *Life After Life*, and other studies of the near-death experience, the being who appears to the dying person is almost always surrounded by or bathed in white light. And sometimes, the dying person sees only an orb of light that, nonetheless, is felt to be a Being who loves the person in an unconditional way.

While a personalized Christ figure does not appear to the dreamer in the following Christ encounter, the experience suggests that Jesus' embodiment could appear at any moment. The close connection between the Light and the personified Jesus suggests that the two are perhaps aspects of the same wondrous truth: Jesus is both a radiant consciousness permeating the universe and a person who transcends all of the limits of incarnate experience.

Could it be that those persons who come from non-Christian backgrounds are more likely to experience Jesus in a less personified form? A Jewish woman who respects all religions experienced Jesus coming to her on the rays of the morning sun.

⌒

I have been meditating for thirteen years. Even though I have been born into the Jewish faith and still actively practice Judaism, I am open to all religions and believe in the unity of all people. I also attend the monthly Unity Church meetings because I love singing praises to God. I also write nondenominational devotional hymns myself. I have allowed myself to be open to Jesus' teachings of spreading love and becoming enlightened.

One morning while I was meditating before sunrise, I felt the sun rising in the east as it began to shine through the window. The sun filled my heart with such warmth that it spread throughout my being. As I was filled with this warmth, I felt Jesus arising from the sun within me and spreading his arms wide. Love spread over me and I heard him say to me, "I Am the Way."

This occurred as an internal experience; my eyes remained closed. It was very real, however, for the warmth and love brought such peace to my being.

What it meant to me, though, might be different from what it means to a Christian. I felt it to be the true essence of Jesus' teachings—that we can all reach the at-one-ment with God, as did Jesus, that Jesus and love and enlightenment merge to become one. I did not feel that I was [to become Christian in practice of ritual religion], but to know that Jesus is that pure love and God is that pure love, and we are all meant to grow to be that pure love and become one with all creation. (L.W.)

L.W.'s encounter with a radiant Jesus did not push her in the direction of becoming a Christian. It deepened her convictions about the universality of Jesus' message and how it transcends doctrinal boundaries.

Non-Christians do experience personal Christ figures, however. In A.Z.'s experience, Jesus appeared and identified himself.

Following my graduation from high school, I had my first "mind-blowing" experience. It shook me to the core. I was living in Palo Alto with a number of young men my age while we participated in a sort of live-in encounter group. Needless to say, it was an emotionally intense and stressful time.

One night I had a profoundly numinous dream of being in a dark, primitive room and standing in the shadows against a wall which was lined with black, aboriginal men. In the center of the room was a skylight in the shape of a Christian cross with brilliant sunlight streaming in at an angle from above, creating a brightly lit cross on the dirt floor. I moved toward the light, looked back to where I had been standing, and saw a Madonna-like figure swathed in colorful glowing robes.

I stepped into the light, looked up into it, and suddenly the whole dream exploded into an ineffable sensation of electrical energy cascading through my whole being. White light as bright as the sun poured through me, rending what felt like membranes or veils in the process. The face of Jesus appeared just in front of me, against the background of bright white light, and a voice said, "I am Jesus." I became aware of what felt like my face turning to stone and cracking, and the face in front of me began fracturing.

The whole episode ended just as abruptly as it had begun, and I was left in my bed sobbing in fear and quaking uncontrollably for about fifteen minutes. I had absolutely no idea what hit me but it was not of this world; it was more real than anything I had ever experienced, and it was indescribably powerful.

Having been raised in a household with a Hindu Vedantist father and a spiritually "neutral" mother, I was unprepared to deal with why the image of Jesus, of all people, should come to me in such a profound way. (A.Z.)

In A.Z.'s experience, we can sense just how foreign these experiences can seem when they don't fit into our current beliefs. The experience can be shattering. Everything that we once held true is threatened by the overwhelming authority of the encounter. We can't deny the experience, but we can't integrate it either, at least at first. It seems especially significant that the figure said, "I am Jesus," not "I am Christ." Given his upbringing, A.Z. may have found it comparatively easy to incorporate a vision of Christ in his spiritual framework. In the West, Christ is traditionally regarded as the essential spiritual nature of Jesus the man. From an Eastern point of view, this underlying spiritual identity is one that we all share. It is the ultimate destiny—still unrealized and unconscious in most of us—to which we are all called. But the Being did not make it easy for A.Z. to identify it as only a universal presence or potential: It asserted its humanness, as well, and its historical connection with Christianity. Consequently, A.Z. will no doubt have to deal with the man Jesus one way or another—if not to accept his place in his life, then to argue eloquently for his exclusion.

In the simple statement, "I am Jesus," Jesus challenges A.Z. to examine the importance of the incarnation of spirit into flesh, not just the availability of a universal or cosmic Christ being. Interestingly, this emphasis on the incarnation of God, rather than the transcendent aspect of the Divine, is a central concern and the highest stated aim of Mahayana Buddhism.[3] In that branch of Buddhism, emancipation from earthly life is not considered the paramount goal. Instead, the devotee strives for enlightenment so *that* he or she may manifest, in the body and through the heart, the kind of transformative love that can quicken and awaken other souls to their oneness with God. Many Christians would probably be surprised to find how much this ideal, called the Boddhisattva ideal, resembles the ideal that Jesus expressed so fully with his life.

While the Light experience is also one of the hallmarks of the classic near-death experience, the following near-death experience featured a very human Jesus without the accompanying radiance. This Christ encounter occurred when a young pregnant Englishwoman contracted tuberculosis and became so ill that she was temporarily declared clinically dead.

Although it happened years ago, it is as fresh in my mind as if it were yesterday.

I was in the hospital and very ill, having contracted tuberculosis at work. We had been testing a herd of cattle for the tuberculosis virus, and the pregnant cows came down with disease. As I was also pregnant, so did I. Subsequently, I became so ill that I was pronounced dead at one point, and had a near-death experience before I was "sent back" to continue my life.

During the experience, I saw lots and lots of steps leading up to a building. I'd gotten about halfway up when I was stopped by a man. He wore no white robe, nor did he have wings. This man was so lovely, but there was so much sorrow in his face, so much suffering, as if for all of mankind. He also expressed so *very* much love and compassion. I felt he knew all about me and loved me; but he told me I couldn't go any farther as I still had so much work to do.

This man wasn't white or black, but he had very bronzed skin as if he had been living out in the open and had been in the sun a lot. He wore a robe which I would say was homespun or handwoven. He wore sandals that were just soles with a strap over the big toe. He seemed dusty and weary, but so loving. I have now come to feel that what I saw was the real Jesus.

Afterward, I began searching to know and find everything I could about him—not just what is in the Bible. I was exposed to that as a child and, although I can now read it with a little more understanding, I have been looking for more.

My earth time is coming to an end and apart from missing the family, I am looking toward going back Home. I just hope I can continue to cope with the pain, and not be too much of a burden to others. I have arthritis, angina arteriosclerosis and have had seven major operations—one for cancer, which I now feel is coming back. As he said, I had work to do; but I now understand he also meant *work on myself!* (K.V.D.)

Obviously, K.V.D. has deeply integrated her experience with Jesus into an attitude toward living and dying that is both realistic and fearless. One might have hoped that her encounter would have saved her from undergoing the obvious suffering that she still faces. Arguably, the very illnesses that have plagued her have also served as catalysts for a deeper, more fearless orientation to life. While we might curse the crises that upset our lives and threaten our health, we are nonetheless forced by such problems to go deeper to derive meaning from them in an unstable world. Finally, we may be able to respond as Emerson responded when a man told him that the end of the world was imminent. Emerson calmly replied, "I can live without it." One gets the sense that K.V.D. is a person who can live meaningfully with or without the security that many of us take for granted.

K.V.D.'s account clearly satisfies the definition of a near-death experience as well as the definition of a Christ encounter. Similarly, the following bears the earmarks of a near-death experience. But the witness—a 25-year-old woman—was apparently not under any kind of physical stress.

⌒

I had gone to bed one night and was saying my prayers. I don't know if I drifted off to sleep or not.

I was standing in my living room and heard a loud trumpet sounding; the vibrations seemed to fill everything as though they were making the same sound. There were other people in the room with me and I asked them if they had heard the sound; they said, "No." I knew at that moment it was Archangel Michael's trumpet sounding. All of a sudden, my arms went up (without my doing it).

I started rising up through the room, and right through the ceiling and roof of the house. I kept going higher and as I went up, a white robe came upon me, and all pain and sorrow was left behind. Joy and peace and love came to me. As I looked around, there were other beings rising also. We were going to this White Light where Jesus was.

When I got there I saw him and he told me, "It's not time yet; you have to go back. You have to wait." Then I was back in my front room.

I don't know if I was dreaming or maybe having a near-death experience. But it was wonderful. (G.K.)

G.K.'s radiant encounter with Jesus strongly indicates that what we have called the near-death experience can occur in non-life-threatening situations. Physical trauma, or temporary clinical death, is apparently only one way to get there from here. Surrender of our limited body-based identity can be achieved in less life-threatening ways, such as through yoga, meditation, and prayer. But it is likely that few of us reach this state of surrender short of actually dying. Facing our own imminent demise seems to be a sufficient, but not necessary, avenue for achieving the opening that we need to encounter the ultimate truth of our lives, however belatedly.

Some people seem to have the capacity to "slip the surly bonds of earth" and enter an out-of-body experience without suffering the attendant physical trauma of a near-death experience. The following dramatic out-of-body experience ushered B.S. into an initially lonely but ultimately fulfilling encounter with Jesus.

⁀

In the fall of 1979, when my husband and I were heavily involved in Christian ministry and very happy in what we were doing, I began to have a lot of out-of-body experiences. Finding little Christian-oriented literature that dealt with the experience in a *positive* manner, I chose to claim Jesus' protection and set about learning all I could from these things on my own. I realized that much scriptural revelation comes from such experiences, and I had a deep hunger to know God in a more direct, personal sense.

One night while I had been sleeping, I became aware of the sensation of leaving my body behind and traveling at a great rate of speed to a series of localities where I seemed to be observing fields of crops in various stages of cultivation. There seemed to be modern equipment, such as tractors. This surprised me, as it seemed as if I'd been hopping from one primitive island to another, and I didn't expect to see a lot of modern equipment. Even though I saw houses, I became more and more disturbed that there were no people.

Finally, I was set down in a lonely, isolated area that I sensed was the backyard of my childhood home. However, there were no buildings in sight, and I felt totally abandoned.

Usually my experiences in the out-of-body state were a time of learning. I could usually grasp the "lesson." But this time I didn't understand so I asked God to show me what it was all about. When I received nothing, I began to challenge him and I reminded him about his promise of wisdom to anyone who asked: "If any of you lack wisdom, let him ask of God, that giveth to all men liberally, and upbraideth not; and it shall be given him." (James 1:5) I also reminded him that he wasn't supposed to be a "respecter of persons," and if he could manifest himself to others in dreams and visions, he should be willing to do that for me, too. I began to feel frustration, resentment, rejection, and finally a deep sense of despair.

Several times I tried to return to my sleeping body, but could not. Then, after totally despairing, I felt some intense vibrations and a high-pitched tone. It was almost as if some sensitive electronic equipment was being tuned. The vibrations were emanating from behind me and I felt the presence of someone whom I perceived to be Jesus. Embarrassment and shame at having railed at him competed with my desire to turn around and see him face-to-face.

My great desire to "behold him as he is" won out and I turned—but I didn't see him. Oh, well, I thought, I knew he wouldn't be there. Disappointed, and feeling self-justified, I returned to my self-pity and despair.

Suddenly, there it was again, the vibrations that I knew emanated from him. This time, knowing that he would be there, I turned quickly around. He—Jesus—was just stepping out from behind a large tree.

"You don't look like you're supposed to look," I told him. I was surprised that his hair was so much lighter than I had thought. His eyes were almost green. He was laughing at me with his eyes, much as one who is amused by a small but stubborn child.

"I've been here all along," he said. "Blessed are those who have *not* seen and still believe."

Overwhelmed by a sense of unworthiness and disloyalty, I fell to my knees in repentance before him. "Oh, Lord," I cried, "I'm so sorry that I ever doubted you." He was standing directly in front of me, and I reached out to hold him around the knees. I remember thinking that I knew I was having a vision of Jesus, which was wonderful. But, of course, I knew that I wouldn't be able to feel anything but air when I tried to touch him. But as my arms went around his knees, I was astounded. There was *substance* there! I was having flesh and blood contact with the man Jesus himself.

Again, I sensed his amusement as he reached down and lifted me to my feet. Vibrations or waves of unconditional love and forgiveness flowed from him around me and into my being.

Then putting his arm around me, we began to walk together. He started to explain some things that I needed to know. He started to say, "In the central ocean are seven thousand to eight thousand islands . . ." But as I listened, the words faded out, even though there seemed to be so much that he taught me. The next thing I knew, I was returning to my sleeping body, and I awoke.

Several years later, I met someone who thought the part about the central ocean was a restatement of Jesus' words, "In my Father's house are many mansions." (B.S. #1)

B.S.'s experience is as sobering as it is uplifting. She exhibits all of the impatience and loss of faith that might befall *any* spiritual seeker who, after trying everything to get closer to God, gives in to angry despair when God does not appear willing to make good on his promises. But no matter how much anger and frustration she expresses, Christ still comes to her. His love overlooks those qualities that might otherwise render her unacceptable to any ordinary person. One gets the feeling that her attitude had little, if any, impact on his profound regard for her, even though it might have delayed somewhat his making himself known to her.

Jesus' willingness to make himself known to B.S., in spite of her lack of patience and faith, is by no means unusual in the lives of those who eventually served him so well. For instance, Teresa of Avila had spent years fighting her spiritual calling, wishing instead to pursue the privileged life of a wealthy, beautiful woman.[4] During this struggle, she suffered from a strange disorder that rendered her paralyzed and in extreme physical pain for days. All of this was apparently due to her resistance to God's calling; for, once she submitted fully to her spiritual life, her symptoms disappeared and Jesus appeared to her regularly thereafter for many years.

It might seem puzzling, even unfair, that Jesus would remain extraordinarily available to individuals whose recalcitrant attitudes seem so undeserving of his presence. However, his statement that "many are called, but few are chosen" (Matt. 20:16; 22:14) suggests that for some of us, the unfoldment of our spiritual life may be an inexorable process that carries us along—regardless of conscious attitudes that might seem to disqualify us from being "chosen."

In summary, the awakening Christ encounter typically takes the witness by surprise, even in those rare cases in which the witness actually seeks the experience beforehand. It conveys the sense that Christ *alone* is making the experience happen, that he is taking the initiative to introduce himself for the apparent purpose of bringing into the individual's awareness a relationship that he *already* recognizes.

This implies, of course, that *any* person not currently expecting a Christ encounter might, in fact, be on the verge of having one.

3

PHYSICAL HEALING

AND

CONSOLATION

Two thousand years ago, Jesus became known to people largely through his miracles of healing. Some of the most moving passages in the Gospels record those instances when Jesus relieved the pain, suffering, or lifelong disabilities of the people who came to him for help. These testimonies instill faith in the reader during the most hopeless times. Indeed, his willingness to save his friends and acquaintances from even death itself shows us just how much he cared to minister to the human, as well as the spiritual, needs of those he encountered.

Many of the accounts I have collected suggest that Jesus' healing ministry still goes on. The stories in this chapter concern Christ encounters of people who were facing a physical or medical crisis.

Because these experiences involve specific physical conditions and events, they serve to remind us that the Christ encounter can effect changes in a person's physical as well as spiritual life.

Just as Jesus' acts of healing impressed people who might have otherwise overlooked his spiritual teachings, some of the following Christ encounters—because they have resulted in tangible changes—may assist the reader in accepting the validity of other accounts.

This chapter, however, does not limit itself to accounts in which medical miracles occurred. Just as often, in the face of health or safety crises, Jesus' presence seems to assure individuals that their worries about life-threatening events or ominous medical conditions are unnecessary. As we'll see in these instances, Jesus can serve as a comforter as well as an agent of direct physical change.

PHYSICAL ILLNESS AND HEALING

It is customary to think that Jesus intervenes in the healing process in only rare and extraordinary situations. But in the following account, a woman suffering from a chronic infection experiences, through hypnosis, Jesus' presence as a natural event available to her at any time—if, that is, she can come to expect it.

❦

I had been sick with a low-grade infection for several months. Antibiotics and other attempts at healing had offered only temporary relief. I found myself, again and again, tired and slightly feverish, with pain in my ear or my throat; not sick enough to go to bed but not well enough to function effectively. Exhausted and discouraged, I stopped by a friend's house and complained about my condition. I asked, "Why can't I get well?!"

He was a professional therapist and had recently been trained in hypnosis, so he suggested that we ask my unconscious to answer. I agreed, and he proceeded to induce a light trance. After offering me several images intended, I assume, to encourage relaxation and healing, he said, "And if a healer were to come, you can allow that healer to come now." I thought, "Well, as long as I have a choice, why should I choose anyone other than Christ himself?"

Immediately I found myself in the presence of someone who, yes, wore a robe and had long hair—but the most powerful part of the image was an intense white light that radiated from him, and that seemed to permeate me, vibrating palpably, and soothing me profoundly. I don't remember how long I sat and basked in that energy, but I remember feeling at the time that his presence seemed remarkably accessible. It didn't seem to require any sophisticated preparation or saintliness on my part. I felt that I was entitled to be in his presence and heal if I chose.

My friend gently guided me back to a normal waking state. I no longer felt sick, and the infection did not return in the following weeks and months. I was extremely thankful, and yet, somehow, it did not feel like a miracle. I was left with the distinct impression that we can expect such an experience to happen, if we allow ourselves to expect it. (P.S.)

P.S.'s conviction that the healing experience is available to her and others corresponds with the experience of others who—while they are in the midst of the profound altered state associated with Christ encounters— feel how easy and familiar the experience seems to be. It is as if they are remembering their true natures—a recollection that, unfortunately, fades as time passes. When Betty Eadie, for instance, found herself out of her body for the first time, it seemed natural and familiar:

My first impression was that I was free. There was nothing unnatural about the experience. I was above the bed, hovering near the ceiling. My sense of freedom was limitless, and it seemed as though I had done this forever.[1]

Such experiences awaken such a sense of familiarity that the recipient actually seems *to remember* an easy, open state of mind and heart from some distant, forgotten time. The unfortunate thing, however, is that this memory seems to fade as everyday life reasserts itself. Miracles, apparently, would be easier to come by if we were able to recapture the profound state of openness in which they seem to occur.

The following account involves a two-stage process in which the recipient was first apparently healed of a physical condition, then shown the source of the healing in a dramatic waking vision days later. Here is the experience in A.D.'s own words:

⌒

I fell down a flight of stairs and was injured so badly that my lower spinal column was in almost continuous distress and pain. I had frequent chiropractic treatments for it. Getting in and out of bed became a careful process, and I would be somewhat stiff in the morning getting up. Even so, I rose at 6:30 A.M. for meditation (because it was the least interrupted, quiet time for me) and to prepare breakfast for my husband and children.

This was the pattern of my life for seven years. One evening, my husband stayed up to watch a late TV sports review and I went to bed. I had just changed into my nightgown when I sensed a presence standing close beside me, on my left, and a (male) voice said, "This night, sleep on your stomach, Alice." The voice that spoke my name was as clear and normal as when two persons are in conversation.

I started to protest in a gentle way. "But you know I can't sleep on my stomach!" I said with mock alarm, meaning that my back would become so rigid in the night that I would need help to get out of bed. Yet even as I said this, I obeyed as quietly as a child would and remembered thinking how astonishing that I could do this, and fell into a deep sleep in this manner almost immediately.

Later, in reliving this extraordinary scene in my mind (and I did many times), I recall how amusing it seemed to me—as I was speaking the words—that I would remonstrate with a spiritual being! It still does. It is recounted here as it happened to illustrate how natural the entire incident seemed.

In the morning, just before actually waking, I distinctly felt the touch of hands massaging, manipulating, and pressing lightly on the lower region of my back. I slipped out of bed as though there had never been an injury.

For three full days I was in a silent, prayerful state filled with awe and reverence, consumed with wonder. Whose hands had I felt on my back? Who was it who had healed me?

On the third night, I went to bed a little earlier again. As I closed the door, the entire wall facing me disappeared, and where there had been a large window and tall furniture occupying that wall space, there was now a brilliant panel of light. I stood transfixed, gazing at it. In the center was a figure in full height, with his hands outstretched, palms upward. He was showing me how my back was healed and who had healed me. I say "he" because I knew instinctively it was the voice I had heard earlier, but this time no words were exchanged. The figure appeared to be androgynous, neither male nor female, nor were the hands characteristic of either. The face was so luminous I could not make out the features, but the hair was plainly visible. It glistened with soft brown waves and fell to the shoulder. He wore a single white garment with no apparent seams, reaching from the neck to the floor and covering the feet, with full, open sleeves at the wrist.

He stood like this for several seconds, and then the wall reappeared in the fraction of a moment as inexplicably as it had disappeared moments before. I remained in that state of grace for some time afterward, and even today, more than thirty years later, the event is indelibly etched in my mind and very simple to recall in all its detail.

Since that first remarkable experience, I have received three other instantaneous spiritual healings. . . . More than anything, it has nurtured in me the concept of gratitude.

Of the initial visitation, I have been asked if I thought it was Jesus. I don't know. I'm certain only that it was a Christ-like figure, and am content with that. (A.D.)

The experience of physical healing would have been life-changing all by itself. But then to be shown that the agent of healing was a radiant Being who cared enough to reveal "himself" to A.D. must have curtailed any tendency to explain away the remarkable change as a coincidence. It is as though the Being appeared not just to satisfy A.D.'s curiosity but to leave no doubt in her mind about the source of her healing.

There are many interesting features to this incident, but one aspect is particularly important to consider. In this account A.D. refrains from identifying the radiant figure as Christ or Jesus during the encounter. She is even content after the experience to let the question of identity remain unanswered. Throughout our examination of Christ encounters, we'll encounter again and again this question: Who is the figure, *really*? Even when the witness identifies the Being for us, we are still left wondering, How does one *really* know?

It is interesting that some persons have experienced Christ in both ways—as a very personal Jesus and as an indistinct Being of Light. For instance, M.L.P.—a woman whose very personal encounters with Jesus are included in other chapters—also had a healing encounter with a Being of Light. Despite his indistinct appearance, he loved her personally enough to heal her with his tears.

⌒

I was going through a stressful time and had an excruciating headache. So bad, in fact, that I had wrapped my head in my dark cashmere sweater to try to keep out the light which seemed to hurt my head. My face was uncovered. I had been writhing on the bed, apparently, because I was lying crosswise on the bed, with my head toward the east. The pain was so bad that I felt tears in my eyes. Then I realized that someone was standing at my head, and when I opened my eyes I saw a "shining stranger" bathed in light. He was crying and the tears that fell from his eyes were dropping on my eyes, causing tears that I had thought were my own. In a type of out-of-body experience, I felt myself leave my body and turn to face him. We embraced and together began turning and ascending in a type of dance of mystical union. (M.L.P. #2)

One gets the sense that the Light Being manifested not only to heal her headache but to alleviate the emotional conditions that had produced it. As such, this account also fits into the category of emotional healing.

It is interesting to note that in A.D.'s Christ encounter, she actually had to *do* something for the healing process to occur. A physical application had been necessary. This requirement is reminiscent of Jesus' manner of healing. He would sometimes require the supplicant to perform some physical action as their part of the healing process. For example, in John 9:1–11 we find the story of Jesus' healing of a man who was born blind. Jesus mixed his own spittle with soil to make clay. Then he placed the clay over the man's eyes and gave him a task: Go and wash off the clay from a specific pool. Only when the man did this was he healed. On another occasion, Jesus told ten lepers that he would heal them. He told them to present themselves to the priest so their miraculous healing could be duly acknowledged, according to the Jewish tradition. The healing took place only as they were on their way to see the priest. *And when he saw them, he said unto them, Go shew yourselves unto the priests. And it came to pass, that, as they went, they were cleansed. And one of them, when he saw that he was healed, turned back, and with a loud voice glorified God, and fell down on his face at his feet, giving him thanks* . . . (Luke 17:14–16).

Of course, we are left to wonder what is going on in this story. Does the specific procedure really affect the healing process directly? Or is a cooperative *spirit* needed to allow higher forces to effect the healing? Perhaps it's significant that A.D. had to be willing to assume a sleeping posture that had previously been painful to her. In essence, Jesus required her to make a leap of faith in a very concrete way.

The same pattern can be found in another account, the story of Laura, which was referred to in chapter 1. She, too, was asked to do something that had previously been excruciating. Other aspects of her story parallel the most dramatic New Testament examples of Jesus' healing ministry. Consequently, I feel it is important to include Laura's complete account here in her own words.

⌒

I am now a grandmother, age 62. For many years I never spoke of my Christ experience. I wish now that I had looked up records so today I could have the proof nonbelievers seem to need. Somewhere I know there is some proof in hospital and church records, as I was called the Miracle Child.

Today I can't remember the dates. I was 11 years old (in Ohio). My mother, brother, and I had scarlet fever; my fever escalated and caused spinal meningitis.

My parents had lost everything. My father, a carpenter by trade, had been unemployed for a long time. The state of Ohio paid my hospital bills, even flying in a doctor from Chicago. The part of Ohio State University Hospital that I was in was a building apart from the main hospital with a high fence around it. I don't remember going in, but I remember my father carrying me out.

I remember one of the nine times that I was held in a tight ball and told not to move, as a big needle was put in my spine. Later, looking in a mirror, for years I could see and count these nine marks. I remember the horrible pain and my thin, twisted legs.

My parents were told my death would be a terrible, screaming thing; best for them not to see or hear, to go home. I lost my sight and hearing but before that, saw my parents, grandparents and Reverend John Lang standing in the doorway of my room, not permitted to come in. The smiles, the thrown kisses, the waving good-bye, I remember and then the sea of pain.

Later, after losing my eyesight, I was lying on my right side. I heard a voice behind me say, "L.B. turn over." I said, "No, it hurts too much to move. You come around to this side of the bed." Then the voice said, "I promise you it will not hurt—turn over." Turning, I saw Jesus. I remember no other words Jesus said to me, yet I know we talked. I watched his beautiful-shaped hand reach out and touch my leg.

Sometime later, I remember remarking to a nurse about what pretty red hair she had. She looked at me in shocked surprise and rushed from the room. The room soon filled up with doctors asking questions. I was a very shy person and there were too many doctors, too many questions. I had to talk about this to Reverend Lang. He was the one person in all the world I wasn't too shy to talk to.

Reverend Lang listened, asked questions, and took many notes. I couldn't see the face of Christ, as it was like looking into a light bulb. But his clothes, the color and material, I had never seen—all that I can remember. I was very blond with very pale skin—the skin of Christ was much darker. The color of a piece of his hair I saw fall on his left shoulder as he reached out his left hand to touch me was a color I had never seen. Reverend Lang called it auburn.

My parents were told I could not live—I did. I was sat in a chair and heard I would never walk—I did. They were told I never would have children—I had three.

I had not seen Reverend Lang for years when I saw in a local paper he was to speak at a church nearby. My sister and I were late so we slipped in a side door. Reverend Lang was speaking about a little girl, "a miracle child," he had known, who had seen and was healed by Christ. Here he was telling hundreds of people of the thing that had happened to me—the things we had talked about long ago. He also said the child had a light about her for days after the visit—something I had not known.

This visit from Christ was never spoken of in my home by my family. I was raised thinking it was something you did not talk about. (L.B.K.)

Laura's account reverberates with the faith-inspiring force of some Gospel accounts of healing. Her experience calls to mind the seemingly hopeless case of Jairus' daughter, whose situation appeared hopeless by the time Jesus arrived to minister to her, but who was nonetheless revived from apparent death (Mark 5:23–43). After Jesus told her parents that she was only sleeping, he took her by the hand and called to her; and she arose. One is also reminded of Jesus' own friend, Lazarus, who was resurrected by Jesus after being dead for days. For myself, I know that after reading Laura's account dozens of times, I am still deeply moved by what happened to her. I cannot help but feel that her account exerts a similar effect on virtually all who read about it.

As we've already noted, the last two stories share a common theme: Both individuals had to have a cooperative spirit and actually *do* something based on faith. Another parallel between A.D.'s and Laura's accounts is the very *appearance* of the Christ figure. For example, both of them saw a being whose face was light itself. But other than the face, they also saw vivid and detailed aspects of his appearance.

Whereas A.D. and Laura received physical healing *themselves* during their Christ encounter experiences, another woman apparently witnessed Jesus healing *someone else*: her mother. This account exemplifies the mediating role that individuals can apparently play through prayer, belief, and love. When K.M.'s experience occurred, she was 25 years old, and her mother was suffering from advanced stages of cancer.

As a child, I used to collect pictures of Jesus and hide them in a box of "treasures." My favorite was one of him on the cross. My aunt, who has cerebral palsy, used to walk me to the Methodist church for Sunday school when I was four, five, and six; and outside of that, I had no real religious background. But I've always believed very sincerely that Christ was there if I needed him.

I elected to be baptized at the age of 12, and my dear aunt was the only person (besides the minister) present. Her faith was her beauty, though outwardly she was not beautiful.

Since both of my parents worked, I was very independent and was never really close to my mother but loved her dearly, even though I felt that she was very detached from us all and never really wanted me initially. I just "happened" to her. Mom and Dad fought often and not casually, and I was always throwing myself in the middle. Often alcohol was to blame, and on my mother's day off from work, she would get drunk to forget what might have been.

After I graduated from college and was teaching high school English, my mother had her first cancer operation—a mastectomy. She had had this tumor for over a year without doing anything about it. She had undergone chemotherapy and the prognosis was not good. After a second operation to remove her lymph nodes on the same side, her outlook was dismal. I was determined that I could save her life through prayer and calling on Christ for help.

I prayed desperately for his help and even offered to trade places with her. I would cry myself to sleep praying. One night, I awoke about 3 A.M. and sat up in bed. I was in my bed, but my bed and I (and my dear sleeping husband) were in my mother's bedroom where she lay sleeping. I was aware that Christ was in the doorway, as if he hadn't just arrived but had always been there. I was in awe—a part of a dramatic play, like an actor, yet a member of the audience, watching, waiting, holding my breath.

The room grew bigger in size and clearer as Christ moved toward my mother's bed. The light was so intense—like sun glinting on the crystals of newly fallen snow—that it hurt deep in my eyes to look, and I realized that part of that pain was my grief for my mother. Silently, gracefully, he walked (glided) to her bedside and touched the side of her face and then turned and nodded. He gazed at me, acknowledged me, and left through the same door. I woke up and it was morning. For the first time, I was at peace knowing that Christ had intervened for my mother and that she would live. I told my mother and father this years later, but somehow I don't feel that they believed its validity. Mom is still alive today. (K.M.)

This story presents a dilemma as we try to understand what happened. K.M. showed a deep love for her mother and a willingness to offer herself as a sacrifice for a woman who had given her little in the way of love when she was a child. The problem is evident if we consider the modern-day emphasis on overcoming the effects of living with alcoholic parents. Children of alcoholics tend to try to keep the peace at a great cost to themselves. They try to win love from someone who, at the time, cannot give it. Modern treatment of "adult children of alcoholics" has focused on differentiating them as individuals from the family. Using this therapeutic approach, they work through the anger of having been abandoned by the addict, and address their own long-neglected needs for nurturance and love.

Perhaps K.M. had completed this psychological and emotional work prior to her attempt to intercede on her mother's behalf. On the other hand, it would be easy for a traditional clinician to interpret her attempts as weakness or "codependency." K.M. seemed to try to glue a shattered world together for her mother rather than admit her own limitations to take care of her mother. K.M. seemed to avoid the affirmation of her own needs.

And yet, this rather clinical assessment is stood on its head by the consequences of K.M.'s loving intercession. That which seems totally unexpected happens—completely beyond what a psychotherapist like myself might anticipate. Obviously, whatever interpersonal problems existed between K.M. and her mother posed an insignificant obstacle to the healing process. This surprising result simply shows how difficult it can be to make an important distinction: What's really the difference between *unhealthy* self-sacrifice on the one hand, and on the other, a *transcendent gift* of the highest form—giving one's life for another person?

This distinction may, ultimately, be impossible to make from the outside; what appears to one person as a reasonable sacrifice to make in a relationship may appear self-destructive or "codependent" to someone else. Certainly, one cannot say that Jesus was "taking care of his own needs" as he consented to mistreatment and martyrdom. He was operating from an entirely different viewpoint—one that regarded the substitution of his own suffering for that of others as a much more important concern than his own personal needs. One can say that his profound act of love served a different need.

Is it unhealthy for us, as ordinary individuals, to take on someone else's suffering? Charles Williams, English novelist and philosopher, thought not. Indeed, he made the "law of substitution" the centerpiece in his interpretation of the spiritual path. He believed that the highest form of love was to take another person's suffering onto oneself, just as Jesus did.

> We are to love each other *as* he loved us, laying down our lives *as* he did, that this love may be perfected. We are to love each other, that is, by acts of substitution.[2]

One of the most beautiful and touching examples of apparent substitution is the case of Williams's friend, C. S. Lewis. He married late in life to a woman who was suffering from cancer that had metastasized to her bones. Lewis loved his wife, Joy, so much that he prayed to share her suffering. Soon after, her disease went into a remission that lasted two years, and Lewis began to develop severe osteoporosis—a rare condition for a man.

> During the period of Joy's recovery, he too contracted a bone disease, and although it was not malignant and was soon brought under control he was obliged to live carefully. "I wear a surgical belt and shall never be able to take a real walk again," he told a friend, "but it somehow doesn't worry me. The intriguing thing is that while I (for no discoverable reason) was losing calcium from my bones, Joy, who needed it more, was gaining it in hers. One dreams of a Charles Williams substitution! Well, never was a gift more gladly given; but one must be fanciful."[3]

Lewis and K.M. demonstrated, perhaps, that there is no error attached to sacrifices made in the context of such deep abiding love. In one sense, such love is always potentially, if not actually, self-destructive; for, giving life, rather than preserving one's own, becomes the paramount concern.

Another account illustrates how important it might be to refrain from attaching too much significance to the physical outcome of intercessory prayers.

P.G. was a 33-year-old wife and after-school teacher living in Florida. Her husband was dying of cancer, and she had two experiences with Jesus. In the first one, she saw a vision of him during one of her weekly meditation group meetings. The second encounter was even more dramatic: Christ told her that her husband had been healed. But soon thereafter, her husband died!

⌒

The second time I saw Jesus was in a vision when my husband was sick in the hospital. He had liver cancer and was in a lot of pain. I was getting into my car one day to go to the place where I worked, and I saw a vision with my eyes open of Jesus standing over my husband's hospital bed. He had his arm raised over my husband, as if he was healing him. Then the vision went away. When I got home that night, I called my husband, and he said that his pain had gone away, and that he hadn't had to ask for another pain pill. He didn't understand why, so I told him about the vision. I had a feeling that it really helped him to believe, not that he didn't believe before, but I think it really helped him.

That night as I slept, I heard over and over in my mind that God, Jesus, and I were one and that I could cure Pedro with God and Jesus. I kept saying to myself, "He's cured, and I can do it." This happened three times, and then I woke up. Also, during this time while I was praying for my husband, I kept hearing Jesus say to me that he was healed and that he would be saved. I assumed this meant physical healing.

I was checking on him every half hour, and for some reason something told me to go upstairs. When I did, I found him dying. I took him in my arms and said, "God loves you, Jesus loves you, and I love you." As soon as I said that, he closed his eyes and that was it. I knew that Jesus was right there ready to help him.

I was shocked when he died. It wasn't until that moment that I realized Jesus meant spiritual healing. (1st P.G.)

If there is a life after death, and we make the transition slowly as some traditions contend, the process of healing and awakening may continue beyond the grave. In support of this idea, P.G. continued to have visions of Jesus assisting Pedro in his adjustment to the afterlife.

⌒

A month after my husband, Pedro, died, I had the following experience. One night during the meditation time of our study group, I saw
Pedro and Jesus. Pedro had his eyes closed. He looked like he did the
minute he died. Jesus took him in his arms and carried him to a place
and was with him. I realized that three days passed before Pedro woke
up and was smiling and was happy just like he used to be. The place was
beautiful with Easter flowers, and everything was green. I smelled lily
of the valley flowers.

Even if Jesus manifests principally to heal the spirit, not the flesh, we
must still contend with the apparent fact that he does not present
himself to everyone in need of spiritual healing. Is there a selection
process based on worth or degree of need? Or could it be that such
healing is available to all, but that only a few are open to it? John heard
Jesus say during his Revelation, "I stand at the door and knock." He
did not say that he would enter our lives unbidden.

Another answer to the perplexing question of why only some
people experience Christ encounters was offered by a Christ encounter recipient who believes these divine initiatives may, in fact, come
freely to all of us, but in our preoccupied mind-sets we may fail to
notice them. She wrote, while reflecting on this mystery, "I do not
know why these experiences happened to me. I wonder if all who
Practice His Presence have these 'touches' but are not aware of or
receptive to them."

This woman's view shifts the question of why Jesus does not come
to us to the question of why we do not perceive him. It represents a
shift from a *theological* question about God's will to a *psychological*
question about our limitations—an orientation that is not commonly
taken in the West. Lama Govinda points out that the Judeo-Christian
religion is theologically based; that is, we have focused on the nature of

a separate Deity, his will for us, and his judgment of us. Buddhism, on the other hand, can be seen as a spiritual psychology, which concerns itself with why we do not perceive God abiding within us at all times as our own fundamental natures.[4]

If we adhere only to a theological perspective, we can only ask whether Jesus approves of us and rewards us with his presence. But if we shift to a psychological perspective, we are free to look at why we do not easily perceive the presence of the Divine in any given moment. It also keeps us from erroneously thinking that we have somehow been rewarded when Jesus appears to us.

American-born teacher Da Love-Ananda (formerly known as Da Free John) describes the master's enlightened state as a light in a room.[5] He says that one must only enter the room to enjoy the radiance of the master's love. He says that when we enter the room, we tend to say, from the ego's limited point of view, "The light shines on *me*." But actually it shines on *anyone* who enters in. By accepting this view, we naturally move away from trying to earn God's love and, instead, begin pursuing spiritual practices—such as prayer and meditation—which might assist us in opening the door to what is always there awaiting us.

REASSURANCE IN A HEALTH CRISIS

Not every encounter with Christ promises a miraculous cure that would astound the patient's physician. Instead, the experience may come to bring reassurance that the healing process will be successful, even with the assistance of modern medicine.

For example, D.T. was a 42-year-old woman who worked as a secretary. By her own admission she had an exceptional need for comfort and reassurance as she faced a serious health condition. Fearfully anticipating oral surgery, she perceived Christ coming to her as a comforting presence.

⌒

I was told last year by my dentist that I had to have all my teeth removed, and as I was allergic to all the local anesthesia, the doctors decided to give me a general. Even though I had had a general once with no problems for one extraction, it was years ago, and I have since had so many life-threatening reactions to drugs that I was terrified by the thought of this operation.

I was thinking about this one evening as I walked home from work, and I suddenly became aware of a presence by my right hand. I turned to look, but there was no one there. The feeling grew stronger, and I felt I could see a figure like Christ walking along by my side. A great feeling of peace and calm filled my being, and all my fear was washed away. I felt a firm conviction that nothing would happen to me, and that even if it did, I would be in good hands. This strong presence stayed with me for a few days, and gradually faded. Although I had moments of nervousness about the impending operation it did not last long, and the memory of that experience kept me cheerful and free of fear through the whole thing.

The presence has returned once since then, and even when it is not there I feel as though it will be if I need it, and that is very reassuring. (D.T.)

Events in the life of M.E. also illustrate this reassuring presence. She was in her seventies, living in retirement with her husband in Arizona. Her husband developed bladder cancer and began following recommended medical treatments that offered good prospects for recovery. Her experience came at what was surely a difficult and tense time.

⌒

In April 1989 my husband was to have bladder surgery. We had been told that the tumors were malignant. The afternoon before his surgery, I was resting in our room. All of a sudden—I must have been praying—I looked toward the windows. On the curtain to the right was the form of Jesus. He didn't speak. I was spellbound. Slowly he faded away. He was, of course, reassuring me of his care and the healing of my husband.

I have looked often at the same area of the curtain, but he has not returned there. He has not needed to.

Well, I am just so very blessed and I know not why! Perhaps many others are touched in this way but do not tell others. (M.E.#1)

Here we see Jesus manifesting to reassure and comfort M.E. and possibly to indicate the imminent healing of her husband.

The experiences cited thus far in this chapter clearly indicate that Jesus manifests in some situations to heal life-threatening medical conditions. In other situations, he seems to come to console and support those who are afraid, either for themselves or for their loved ones. But we are left wondering why such interventions seem so rare. In fact, for some people it might be easier to accept the premature death or the suffering of their loved one if God *had never* been known to intervene at all. When we are faced with compelling evidence that God does occasionally manifest in this way, it can be deeply disheartening. We can be shaken by our apparent powerlessness to orchestrate such interventions. We might find ourselves asking, Why are *our* prayers not good enough? Why do the people in our lives seem to suffer and die without the slightest token of assistance from above? Instead of serving to deepen our faith, Christ encounters that grant a few individuals a reprieve from death have the potential to awaken our anger and cynicism toward God's apparent capriciousness.

But maybe Jesus comes principally to heal the spirit, not the body. Maybe in some cases the body responds also and provides an additional effect to which we may tend to attach greater importance than is warranted. Given the fact that all of us are mortal—that death is only more or less imminent—maybe Jesus comes to correct more serious conditions than illnesses and injuries. Perhaps the primary focus for his healing is our need for love and redemption.

This idea gains support from the story of R.H. whose wife was dying from cancer. In their search for medical alternatives they had joined a weekly study and meditation group. Eventually, as his wife grew weaker and weaker, the group began to meet at their home. Finally she was so weak that she could only participate from her own bedroom while the rest of the members met in the living room. R.H. remembers:

At the close of one of our meetings, I went in to see my wife after all the other members had left. She looked radiant. I immediately asked her what had happened, and she told me, "Oh, Jesus has just been here. He said that he'll come for me tonight at 3 A.M. Isn't it all wonderful?" She still seemed to be in an ecstatic state of joy. Such a statement of impending death seemed not to faze her a bit. I went on to bed in a separate room where I had been sleeping since her nights had become so restless with the illness. I set my alarm to wake me just before 3.

When I awakened at that early morning hour, I went in very quietly to her bedside and sat down to watch her. At exactly 3 she stopped breathing and passed on. (R.H.)

Most of us experience a wide range of contradictory emotions when someone we love is suffering from a protracted and apparently terminal illness. Above all, perhaps, is a feeling of helplessness. Consequently, R.H. must have experienced a great deal of comfort knowing that Jesus assisted his wife in her time of greatest need when he, himself, could do nothing. In that sense, the Christ encounter was meant for him, too.

Indeed, when Jesus manifests during the final hours of a person's life, everyone around the dying person seems to partake of his influence. In the following account, B.G.'s dying father alone sees Christ in the room while his family attends to him. But B.G. and his mother have their own experiences that supplement and verify his father's vision.

My father was in the hospital and near death. On Wednesday at 5 P.M., he actually died and was resuscitated. At 9 P.M. he died again and was resuscitated. Then, in the early morning hours on Thursday, he had a seizure and was stabilized. At 6 A.M. the doctors called to have us come in. When we arrived my dad was conscious and alert but on a respirator. He was pointing at the ceiling. The nurse who was there said nothing, but we knew Dad was having a spiritual vision. I asked him if he saw someone. Dad nodded yes. "Is it your mother?" I asked. By squinting, he gestured no. "Is it a relative?" Again he indicated, no. Then I asked, "Do you feel love, light, and acceptance?" He responded with a glowing yes. "Is it Christ?" *Yes, Yes!* He nodded.

He pointed at me, then at my mother, extended two fingers in a V and brought them together. He then crossed his heart and pointed to the figure. I knew he was asking me to promise in front of God that I would take care of Mom.

Dad began breathing easier, so the doctors removed the respirator tubes. Then, on Saturday morning, my mother and I both awoke with the same dream: Two men dressed in white were assisting Dad to sit up. The only difference was in Mom's dream she was lifting his legs.

When we called the hospital, they said he slipped a little during the night but was resting comfortably. But at 8:00 or so, he passed over.

Dad's funeral was on the following Tuesday. I had not been a practicing Catholic for thirty years. When it came time for

Communion I heard my father's voice say, "Come have supper with me." (B.G.)

R.H. and B.G. had reassuring and possibly life-changing experiences associated with the Christ encounters of their dying loved ones. But the intensely meaningful experiences were not sufficient to reverse the dying process.

Given how most of us fear death and the loss of those we love, it might be hard to accept that Christ would manifest at all without actually reversing the illness that has befallen us or the one we love. We would like to have more than consolation—we would like to *survive*. But none of us can escape our destinies as mortal beings. Even Jesus' companions gained no permanent advantage over death. Indeed, legend tells us that all but one of the disciples experienced harsh deaths.

Again and again history suggests that the Divine only rarely seems to alter the material conditions we face. And yet, we can perhaps take heart that his love insulates us against the doubts and fears that prevent us from marshaling our best efforts in the face of adversity. Beyond that, it may also be true that the Divine will assist us—as he did R.H.'s wife and B.G.'s father—in the final transition from this world to the companionship he has promised.

4

EMOTIONAL

HEALING

A single theme unifies this otherwise diverse collection of Christ encounters. In virtually every case, the Christ figure expresses *profound love* for the person he meets. The way this love affects the person seems to depend on his or her needs at the time. For instance, we have already seen that if a person is ill, the Christ encounter can promote actual physical healing or facilitate the graceful acceptance of the sickness or dying. As we'll see in the accounts that follow, the same intercessory process promotes mental and emotional healing. In a span of moments, the Christ encounter can lift a person out of emotional turmoil, freeing him from paralyzing emotions and empowering him to undertake new directions in life. The healing seems to take place as the witness recognizes that she is loved and accepted by a radiant Being who *knows her completely* and who points to a relationship with himself as a completely sufficient refuge for the "poor in heart."

The reader will observe in the following cases that an intensely personal relationship with Jesus develops in virtually every one. It is as though the emotional problems—often precipitated by interpersonal conflict or loss—could only be healed through a deeply personal connection to someone who would never fail the witness. Whether one turns to Jesus, or some other personal embodiment of unfailing trustworthiness, it is likely that in moments of despair and loneliness, each of us discovers that we need God to become human for us.

THE HEALING OF DEPRESSION AND FEAR

J.D.'s experience came to her during a period of deep depression. Despite her emotional state, she said she had gradually developed a relationship with Jesus over a period of months prior to her intense and momentary encounter. In her experience, and in many others, Christ encounters occur as punctuation in an ongoing relationship with him, rather than as an event unrelated to the witness's prior beliefs and yearnings.

After years of searching all types of religions and beliefs, I came home to Christ. He is the being that I am most culturally and emotionally able to understand. About eight years ago, he reached out to me and I answered. I'm vague on that first experience. I can't put it into words. It came over time. It was not a bright light experience. It was a relationship that grew, and after a while I looked back and realized that he was real for me.

Then he came to me in an appearance that was sudden, intense and brief. I was in one of my depressions—one of my crying jags when I felt totally worthless and unloved, self-hating, and alone. In my black pit there was suddenly a window thrown open and love and light streamed down on me. I saw the Christ and he said to me, "You are loved." It was there for one clear instant and then it was gone and I was reeling from it. The depth of my being felt changed and I have since felt an inner confidence in the love that is there and in the certainty of Christ's reality. (1st J.D.)

J.D.'s momentary encounter left her with an enduring sense of Jesus' love for her. Obviously, the length of the encounter had little to do with the impact it had on her life. We might ask, Why do these encounters have such a lasting therapeutic benefit?

We can answer this question, at least in part, with some theories on the process of psychotherapy and why it works. Several leading spokesmen—including Carl Roger[1] and M. Scott Peck[2]—believe and assert that "unconditional positive regard," or the underlying assurance that one is accepted or loved, is the principal healing force in the therapeutic process. My own experience as a psychotherapist bears this out. It makes sense when we consider that most emotional problems develop around a conviction that one is not loved—and not even worthy of love for that matter.

But while I usually find it possible to express unconditional positive regard for my clients, it is no easy matter to convince some of them that they are *worthy* of love. Why? Because in most cases, they know things about themselves that they feel invalidate another person's love for them. And they are likely to feel that the other person will cease loving them once the whole truth is known. They might think, "I've fooled them and it's just a matter of time before I'm found out." This feeling of unworthiness of love can be overcome in the therapeutic process, because the therapist acts as a confessor who still accepts the person, even when he knows the "sins." This acceptance is healing.

In most cases, the Christ encounter transcends this personal dilemma. Consider what happened to J.D. She was somehow able to grasp the immediate fact that Jesus' love is based on a complete knowledge of her. His love is profoundly healing because it is a "fully informed" love.

Another woman found that Jesus' love did not diminish as he left her, even though she dreaded to see him go. The witness—a 44-year-old woman—had the following dream twenty years ago.

⁓

I once had a dream of Christ, too. It is one of the focal points in my life. It has carried me through many a dark and frightening hour.

He was in New Jerusalem, attending to a group of people, in a balcony-like area. He came to me and did not speak. But with his mind, he told me he loved me, oh, so much. I did not speak either, but felt if he should move on to other people, I would die. I couldn't bear to have so much love taken from me.

I didn't die when he moved on. His love left an indelible mark upon me and I turned to talk with the others.

Christ's beauty and serenity were indescribable. (S.L.)

S.L.'s experience brings to mind the resistance many of us have to entering into intensely loving relationships: We fear the eventual loss of the love. Believing that love is exclusive, we feel that if the other person moves on, we will be left with nothing. Given the way many relationships go, this fear is a reasonable one. However, S.L. discovers that Jesus' love sustains her even as he attends to others. She learns that his love for her is *deeply personal, but not exclusive.*

Many of us have done something in our past that we cannot forgive ourselves for. The passage of time may take the edge off of our regret and even render it tolerable, but some of these memories remain largely untouched by time. No matter how many people around us try to alleviate our guilt and remorse, no matter how much we might try constructively to "reframe" our act in a way that makes it understandable if not forgivable, we may still hold ourselves accountable for something that apparently cannot be undone. When we cannot forgive ourselves or accept the atonement available from our peers, ministers, counselors, or society in these intransigent situations, we seem to require an intervention beyond the realm of ordinary healing processes.

P.G.'s experience demonstrates how a Christ encounter can begin to usher a person beyond seemingly inescapable guilt and sorrow. Today, P.G. is a 32-year-old artist and mother of three, but at the age of 19, she experienced a sense of deep healing after having an abortion.

⌒

About twelve years ago, circumstances seemed to force me into a corner and I made the decision to have an abortion, which devastated me. A couple of days after the abortion, I went to an afternoon movie trying desperately to run away from my thoughts. I ended up leaving the theater abruptly in the middle of the show and going for a drive into the country, crying while simultaneously singing "In the Garden." I became aware of a bright light filling the car. It was as if a huge flashlight was shining from above and the beam of bright light was following me down the road. I sensed the presence of Jesus so strongly sitting beside me that I kept looking for him in bodily form. When the light left, I felt calmed, restored, and forgiven. (2nd P.G.)

So many of us labor under the emotional consequences of actions that we cannot undo. P.G. experienced what is perhaps the only solution for such unrelenting regret—that God loves us *anyway*. C.M. faced a similar dilemma, except that the so-called "unforgivable" action was her father's own suicide.

⌒

It is hard to imagine that out of a great tragedy such as a parent taking his own life great joy and peace can come, but that is what happened to me. At the age of 57, my father committed suicide by shooting himself in the head with his shotgun. I was at the funeral home and had just spent some quiet time with him before getting ready for the funeral. It was hard enough to lose my father, but to lose him in this way was almost more than I was able to stand. After the first shock of hearing what had happened, I was trying to deal with what for me had come to be the hardest part. Because he had taken his life, I knew that he could not go to heaven. At least, this is what I had been taught, and it was hard to try to come to terms with that. I was struggling with this as I walked down the hall toward the chapel for my father's service. Just before I got to the chapel, a little voice that I now call my "knowing" said to look up, so I did.

There about six feet off the floor, floating toward the ceiling, was my father and Jesus Christ with their backs to me. They were hand in hand and seemed to be walking up and out the ceiling. As I looked at them, they turned their heads and both smiled at me. There was a bright light all around them, and there was the most wonderful feeling of love and peacefulness about them and in me. I knew at that moment that my father was going to be with God, and that he was happy and at peace. Then they disappeared in a fine mist.

I was able to go in to that service with a smile on my face and peace in my heart.

After this experience, I knew that what I'd been taught was wrong, and it would be up to me to seek out my own way to reach and serve God. (1st C.M.)

It seems ironic that the very experience that releases C.M. from the belief her father cannot be forgiven also precipitates a spiritual crisis for her: It forces her to go beyond her religious indoctrination to find her own path to God. Given the loneliness and interpersonal strife that can easily accompany such a personal journey, one can understand why individuals might unwittingly prefer *not* to encounter a Being whose all-embracing love might compel them to question restrictive, but widely accepted, beliefs and doctrines. And yet, it was this embracing love that repeatedly took Jesus beyond the social and religious customs of his day—a love that forgave prostitutes, that healed on the Sabbath, and that ultimately sought forgiveness for even those who killed him.

THE HEALING OF RELATIONSHIPS

Interpersonal relationships are a primary source of emotional turmoil, so it's not surprising that many of the accounts of emotional healing by Jesus are related to this area. Many people grow up in such turmoil that they enter adulthood fearing that they will never find anyone who will stand by them. These feelings sometimes prevent them from ever taking the necessary risks to find out if an enduring relationship is even possible. In the following account, Jesus appears to a girl experiencing anxiety about her life, and reassures her about her future.

☞

When I was a teenager I had an encounter with Christ. Although I had a loving and supportive family, I had troubled teen years. I had the habit of praying every night before I went to sleep. One night, as I was praying, the face of Jesus became so vividly imprinted in my mind, that I was compelled to open my eyes, and sure enough, there was Jesus in the corner of my room! I could only see his face. His lips didn't move, but he 'told' me not to worry—that I would have a husband, one son and one daughter. He also said that I would have a white house in town (I was living on a farm), and my husband would have a blue-collar type of job, and we would be very happy.

Now I know this sounds completely senseless! But I cannot begin to explain the peace and joy and sense of relief that I felt inside of me. Those feelings are inexpressible! When I boarded the school bus the next morning I wanted to shout that I had seen Christ! But, I didn't of course, because I would have been laughed at. I have never told anyone of my encounter. It still sounds crazy to me, but I know it happened. Without a doubt I know that.

A couple of years later I married a boy that I knew was for me from the time of our very first date. Five years later we adopted a baby girl, and two years after that we adopted a baby boy. My husband was in blue-collar work the first twenty-five years of our marriage, attempted white-collar management, but failed for very strange, unusual, and unforeseen circumstances. After much personal stress, he is back in blue-collar work and much happier. The first home we lived in was white, although when we had our children, our home was another color.

We have been married thirty-three years, and although our later years have been a little less than happy, we had an unusually happy life when our children were young.

Christ has never appeared to me again in that way, but I know, now, how wonderful it will feel to meet him at the end of my life on this earth. (A.R.)

As a counselor, I know that the foreknowledge Jesus conveyed to A.R. would greatly assist some of my clients who have been so wounded by relationships that they have become fearful and even cynical. While it is easy to understand why Jesus' appearance might not be needed by those who are still strong enough to take risks and grow through the process, it is easy to see why his presence might be considered the "treatment of choice" when unrelenting hopelessness sets in.

Another woman received similar assurances when she, too, began to feel hopeless about relationships with men.

☞

On Mother's Day, I went to church and was kneeling before the Blessed Mother. I told her that I was so tired of meeting the wrong men, and that I wished to meet the right man for me. While I was praying and crying, Christ appeared beside me. He was dressed all in white. He put his arms around me and said, "Everything is going to be all right now, everything is going to be all right."

I went home knowing that the right man was coming. (C.W.)

C.W. had no doubt that Jesus' words would come true in a literal way. While there's no way of knowing whether his words referred to an eventual relationship, C.W. elected to interpret them that way. She did everything she could to prepare for the meeting that she was convinced would soon happen. It didn't happen instantly: Actually, she met her future husband at a wedding some time later. But throughout, C.W.'s faith never waned. She said, "Once or twice since then I've said to myself, 'Did this really happen?' But he was there with me. . . . I believe he was physically in the room with me."

Individuals who have been mistreated as children frequently find that they end up in similarly abusive relationships as adults. As children, they were unable to understand that their parents had a problem, so they took the responsibility upon themselves, thinking that if they could only be better, the anguish would stop. Consequently, as adults, these individuals may too readily accept the familiar abusive treatment that can come from bosses, lovers, or spouses. It's at this point that a Christ encounter can have a potent, transformative influence. For example, a 44-year-old divorcée experienced a renewed belief in herself in the following Christ encounter.

☞

I was the typical product of a severely dysfunctional family, in which I experienced physical and emotional abuse. I had absolutely no confidence in myself at all by the time I had grown up. I had no education either. I was attracted to an abusive man who withheld affection. All I ever knew is that I was in pain. I never felt I had any control over my life. My husband spent the marriage trying to convince me I was ugly, stupid, and crazy. I shudder now at the passive role of victim I played.

A friend introduced me to a book, *The Story of Jesus*, by Jeffrey Furst. I started to feel there was light at the end of the tunnel. My husband's behavior, however, became increasingly more depressing. I wanted some love and joy in my life. I was desperately searching for a way out of my relationship with my husband. I wanted joy and peace.

One night I had a dream. Jesus came to the end of my bed—I did not see his face. I do remember being fascinated by the intricate herringbone pattern to the weave of his garment. It was a lovely glowing light-oatmeal color. He said, "There is joy in Christianity." And at that instant my whole being was pervaded with an intense feeling of ecstasy. I remember thinking that this was the way I was supposed to feel. I could never find the words to describe the way I felt.

I awoke completely amazed at the experience and I knew something extraordinary had happened. I couldn't really believe that Jesus had heard my prayers or come to a nonentity like me. I went to a priest I knew and trusted. He said I should believe I had experienced an actual encounter with Jesus and that I was very blessed indeed.

I can see now how this encounter became a catalyst in my life. I realized if Jesus had enough esteem of me to visit me personally, then I really did exist on an equal basis with all other souls.

I went back to school for five years and became a registered nurse. My husband and I were eventually divorced. I went into therapy and started to deal with the childhood abuse that almost destroyed me. I have since forgiven my parents and am actively working at trying to have a better relationship with them. (G.P.)

Letting go of a long-standing but unhealthy relationship can be especially difficult for individuals like G.P., who often feel obliged to make their relationships work at any cost to them. And yet, once G.P. realized that Jesus loved her, her belief in herself was greatly restored. She was eventually able to develop in her own right and emancipate herself from a relationship that had become a form of imprisonment.

Another woman who was abused as a child experienced several Christ encounters. Most of them seemed to result in the healing of insecurity and anxiety—emotions that had their roots in her experience with overly critical parents.

☞

I was having a terrible time. I was very nervous because of several unpleasant experiences. Then, one night I dreamed I was in the backyard and I saw Christ walk through the gate. I was overjoyed to see him and ran over to hug him. We hugged for a while and then he started to pull away, but I wouldn't let him go. He said that I had to let him go, so I did.

A few weeks later I was thinking how comforting that dream had been, but so very brief—I wished he had stayed a longer time in the dream. That night I dreamed of a spiritual Being standing in the yard at the side of the house. This Being sparkled and shone as if made out of thousands of brilliant diamonds—I couldn't even make out any features, just an outline of diamonds from head to toe. This Being said, "Don't worry, Christ will be coming to talk to you again."

Since then, I've had several other dream and waking experiences with him.

On one occasion, I was feeling very depressed and down on myself, feeling that I couldn't do anything right. Suddenly I felt his presence in the room. I couldn't see anyone, but I knew it was him. He said that I shouldn't allow *anyone* to make me feel bad about myself or criticize me. He sounded angry, but I knew the anger wasn't for me, but for the way I had been hurt.

Another time, I wasn't thinking of anything in particular, when I heard a voice say, "Child, I am always with you." (R.R.)

As a therapist familiar with the lifelong effects of child abuse, I interpret the significance of this story to be that Jesus has given R.R. the very thing she never had: He has expressed his love for her and reassured her, again and again. He has assured her that he will always be with her. Sometimes we forget just how essential basic assurances of love can be in the healing of long-standing wounds.

K.S. was 22 and in a troubled relationship when she had her Christ encounter. It gave her the reassurance she needed eventually to end the destructive relationship.

∽

I had been involved with a man for most of my teen and adult years, and the relationship had not been a healthy one for me or him. Over the years, we had grown apart. I was looking for the answer to how to end the relationship, or if I should end it. One day, my boyfriend and I went bow hunting deep in the woods. I was not hunting: I merely wanted to be with him, and to enjoy nature. My boyfriend brought me to a hunting blind made of rocks and told me to stay there until he came back, for my own safety.

I had little with me to entertain myself—just a backpack with some food and apple juice. So I engrossed myself in a study of nature. I really looked at the colors of the leaves, the insects crawling near me, and the glorious blue sky.

At one point, I was meditating on the troubles of my relationship with my boyfriend. I looked up at the sun, partially hidden behind leaves, and it seemed to pulsate. I saw a face in the sun that resembled Christ. Being cautious, when I heard a voice speak to me, I asked,

"Who are you?" The light vision pulsated and answered, "Some call me Buddha, some call me Christ." I said, "I don't know Buddha." And he answered, "Then I am Christ." I looked over at my boyfriend, who was passing by, and I felt love for him but felt detached from him. I don't recall most of my conversation with Christ, but I know I spoke of my fear of leaving my boyfriend, of "failing" my boyfriend, of being alone if I left him. The one phrase that I remember distinctly is Christ saying, "I am with you always."

That phrase, that voice, that face, have been a great source of comfort to me in the years since then. I have finally freed myself from that unhealthy relationship. As of yet, I have not found a new love, but I am confident that he is out there. And that *He* is out there to be with me always as He promised His apostles and me, as lowly as I am.

If you would like to know some background, I am a Roman Catholic, I currently teach preschool and Sunday school. I attended Catholic school grades one through ten. I am not a holy person and I don't know why Christ came to me, except to remind me that I need not fear loneliness, for we are never alone if "I am with you always." (K.S.)

Jesus doesn't say to K.S., "You don't need men, only me." He lets her know that whatever happens, his love will not abandon her. Obviously, he offers a *different kind* of relationship in which K.S. can find the security often lacking in ordinary human relationships.

The Being's answer to K.S.'s question, "Who are you?" underscores our difficulty in conclusively identifying the Being who appears in some of these encounters. The Being does not say that he is Christ *or* Buddha: He implies that he is both at the same time. From one point of view, it is tempting to conclude that this Being has no intrinsic nature—that he is a spiritual chameleon who only mimics the beliefs of the witness.

However, perhaps we are making a virtue of our own inability to experience ourselves as multifaceted beings. Instead of seeing this Being as having no stable identity we would do well to consider that the Being's vast inclusiveness allows for many names.

Of course, we as individuals build our identities by excluding aspects of ourselves until we arrive at a suitably pared-down version of who we *think* we are. Much of this takes place in childhood under the influence of our parents' values and injunctions. We learn what to express and what to suppress to gain their acceptance. Later in life, if we do the work we need to do, we begin to recover those important aspects of ourselves that we cast off in our attempts to be good children. As we regain our own vital wholeness through this reclamation project, we might find that a Being's claim to be two persons at once may not seem as puzzling or as impossible as it once did.

In an account similar in effect to K.S.'s, a 32-year-old woman was feeling the loneliness that comes from knowing that an emotional involvement is over when Jesus manifested to remind C.A.M. of His enduring love for her.

❧

I was at a very low point at the end of an intense personal relationship. My friend was throwing a "welcome to spring" party at our apartment one Friday night, and I knew it would be too wild for my frame of mind. I, therefore, made arrangements to stay at a hotel for the night.

I settled in for the evening, complete with book, food and TV. As I compared the differences in my emotions now with when I first met my friend, the most glaring awareness was "I'm alone again. I'm alone again, and I've accomplished nothing. Here I am, right back where I started. Has all that I've gone through here been for nothing?" As I sadly thought this, the room changed subtly. A feeling of utter peace descended on me, and the area to the left of the balcony and sliding glass doors brightened. I felt a presence fill that area and a feeling of being absolutely loved filled me, swept over me. I knew it was Jesus. I mentally heard a voice say, "You are not alone. You have me." We communicated, then the Presence withdrew, back out the doors where he had first entered. I was renewed. I should add that the significance of the balcony is that beyond it lies the ocean, which held a lot of meaning for me.

I had a rough time after this but I'm still holding on to the faith this experience instilled within me. From that night on, I feel that the course of my life was redirected, reshaped. I discovered an inner strength that was lacking before I heard the simple declaration, "You are not alone." (C.A.M.)

Besides providing the emotional support individuals usually need before terminating a destructive relationship, Jesus' intervention can also apparently *improve* a relationship by removing some of the obstacles that stand in the way of deeper trust and intimacy. In the following account, the witness experiences relief in two areas—her fear of the dark and her sexual problems in her marriage.

One cannot deny that sexual relations are of crucial importance in maintaining most healthy marriages. Even so, some might balk at the idea of Christ manifesting to heal sexual dysfunction. Instead of debating this matter, it is best to remember that we can never be sure of Jesus' intention. After all, just because the Christ encounter has a particular effect on the recipient does not mean that the Christ figure intervened *only* to address that condition. On the basis of dozens of Christ encounters included in these chapters, all we can really say with confidence is that the Christ figure expresses an almost overpowering love for each recipient. Perhaps we experience healing wherever it is needed, whenever we experience such profound and total love. M.M.'s sexual feelings during the encounter were, from this standpoint, merely the indication of where the healing was needed.

⌒

I joined a charismatic prayer group at a time when I was open to my spiritual life. I was in a state of excitement and grace while at the same time aware of a spirit of fear.

I felt this fear at night when I would walk from my room toward my newborn daughter's room down the hall at night to nurse her. It was a fear of the dark and an "evil" presence.

I was also in the process of deep contemplative and persistent prayer requesting God for a healing that would positively affect my sexual relationship with my husband.

One morning about 4 or 6 A.M., I "awoke" to a feeling that penetrated my very being with a warmth and a joy that was overwhelming. I opened my eyes and saw Jesus "hovering" or floating before and above me as I lay on my bed. His arms were stretched out and opened—as if welcoming me or blessing me.

I recall vividly the love in his face. I felt I was looking at his face with my soul. His face and upper body were visible and translucent, but his body was covered in a flowing robe.

Love was radiating from his face into my body and I felt it physically as warmth and glow and throbbing vibrations. The best way to explain it in human terms would be a spiritual-sexual experience.

Since then, my fear of the dark has lessened and I have come to realize that I am capable of experiencing orgasm. I do not know if there is any connection between my experience of Jesus and my prayers in this regard. (2nd M.M.)

M.M.'s encounter with Jesus apparently healed her on at least two levels. And yet, not a word was spoken. The evidence of his love was, once again, completely sufficient to activate the healing process.

———

Sometimes relationships end without any closure when two persons part ways without one of them letting the other know the full truth of their feelings and their reasons for leaving. For years thereafter, it may be hard for those who were left behind to let go and move on, as we wonder whether we did the right thing, or whether we could have done something different. This rehashing can prevent us from moving forward into new relationships.

In the following encounter, Jesus manifests ostensibly to assure the recipient that she had done well in a relationship in which the other person had apparently left before she could arrive at any closure.

⌒

I had my second Christ encounter following a relationship with a man who hurt me very deeply.

During our relationship, I put my own pain in the back of my mind and took care of him, for he was in very bad shape psychologically. After he left I had doubts. I knew I had done the right thing, but I wondered if I had done enough.

About this time, I had a dream in which I was walking along the Sea of Galilee. The Master approached me and he took something—I don't know what it was—and pinned it on my lapel, right above my heart. What I remember distinctly was the ring on his hand. It was gold with a square and in the square were sixteen round amethysts. It seemed there was assurance I had done well in that relationship. I just remember looking at that ring as he was pinning on the object.

Years later the man came back to me and said he was sorry for what he had done. (R.J.#2)

R.J. experienced Jesus' gift as a symbol of completion, which freed her to let go of the old relationship. This dream brings to mind the importance of rituals and ceremonies as a way to signify concretely the end of a learning process and the inauguration of a new phase.

Recognizing the power of such enactments, many modern psycho-therapists assist their clients in setting up such rituals in order to obtain closure in a relationship with a person who has disappeared or died. Depending on an individual's need, anything from writing letters to addressing the deceased at the gravesite can serve as effective ways to obtain closure when the other person is unavailable for one reason or another.

THE DARK NIGHT—A MEANINGFUL ORDEAL BROUGHT ON BY SPIRITUAL AWAKENING

Sometimes when we adopt new, higher ideals or affirm a closer, more committed relationship with God, our lives take a turn for the worse before they get better. All of our unfinished business from the past comes back to haunt us—our regrettable choices, hurtful actions, and unresolved pain from old relationships. We find ourselves looking in the mirror at a person who has failed time and time again to respond to a higher calling. This awareness of our shortcomings can make some people hopeless. *We become depressed because we have awakened to our "fallen state."*

J.M.S. experienced Jesus coming to her following her slide into a depression after embarking on what she thought would be an exciting, uplifting spiritual practice.

⤳

I began to meditate and pray, attempting to draw the light of Christ from within myself. In meditation I found warmth and peace of mind, harmony and relaxation. Out of meditation, however, I found myself introspecting and analyzing different areas of my present life with some amount of criticism and negativity. The "snowballing" effect of those few weeks of intense introspection consumed me with depression, doubt, fear, and anxiety. Worst of all, I found myself feeling unworthy of the Father's love.

In the midst of this suffering and burdensome consciousness, Jesus came to me in a concise and vivid dream. I stood in a narrow white hallway with a doorway at the end. Jesus stood in the doorway simply dressed in a simple long white robe, without sash or embellishment. Behind Jesus was a grayness or gray cloud. The very second my eyes met his, he turned. The symbolic movement meant everything to me! The impression I immediately received was "Follow me and have faith." The grayness Jesus turned on to shocked me, for I expected a path paved with gold. But my path with Jesus has its crosses. I believe he appeared to me so I would find strength in him and carry on.

My perception of everything following the dream has taken on a new light in the grayness. My love and spiritual awareness of Our Lord only deepens with time.

The Christ encounter I experienced was not engulfed in light and glory, but the message was clear to me. (J.M.S.)

As we have seen in so many of the Christ encounters, Jesus' appearance signaled a new beginning for J.M.S., even though the path ahead looked nebulous. Interestingly, he does not deny the "grayness" of life, uncertainty, or potential for sorrow but instead calls her to follow him through it. With every significant new beginning, there is a death of old ways of thinking and being—a fact easy to overlook as we contemplate the "good news" of his coming.

Some people who have had Christ encounters have reported feeling so loved by Christ that, after their experience, they were able to weather lengthy ordeals with surprising ease and confidence.

⌒

Some of the darkest times I've faced began with my excommunication from a Christian fellowship due to a misunderstanding, and culminated nine years later when I developed a brain tumor that had to be removed.

During that "dark night of the soul," I had an experience that to me was the most profoundly beautiful experience of my entire life. I remember it clearly because it happened on Valentine's Day.

My husband came to bed well after midnight as is customary. But he proceeded to wake me up to fuss at me about the way I wasn't keeping the house clean. I had a broken ankle and had been scooting around on my fanny, cast and all, to pick up after the children, who should have been doing it themselves.

I'm not a naturally organized or tidy person, and I have to exert real effort to maintain a semblance of order. But the children, after seeing their father's disrespect of me, were being particularly rude to me during that time. However, I was blamed for their behavior, because I "allowed it." I was frustrated and at a low point emotionally because I was physically incapacitated and the situation was totally out of control.

My husband chose that night to tell me that he no longer loved me and that he felt he and the children would be better off without me. I remember asking him if he was willing to try to work things out, and he said, "No."

I got out of bed and hobbled to the living room on my crutches and sank down onto the couch. I know that I cried for several hours until I was totally spent. I told Jesus that my children and husband didn't love me and treated me with great dishonor. I told him that I had no one left but him.

At that moment, I felt the sofa cushion beside me sink down and felt someone sit down beside me. I reached my hand over hoping it might possibly be my husband, but *there was no one there physically.* Then I felt a warm and loving arm go around my shoulder, and was suddenly immersed in the most unconditional love imaginable. I knew that no matter what happened to me, *he was enough.* It was as if I became a totally detached party in the whole situation with my family. I disconnected. I was immediately able to respond with true disinterested love for the first time.

The sense of love and total peace lasted for more than six months without being broken by any situation or person. I knew that I could lose everything physically, but still have everything that mattered—because I had him, Jesus, and that *nothing* and *no one* could ever separate me from his love.

Since that time, in all fairness, I must say that God has been allowed to work out his love in our home and marriage. But there are still times when I yearn for that total completeness I felt when, for a season, he protected me and he was all I had. (B.S. #2)

I grew up in the same small town with this woman, and we went through school together from first grade to graduation. She had never had an easy time of it. She was the kind of person that kids don't particularly respect—too nice, kind of old-fashioned, raised by religiously conservative people. Caught up in adolescent values, I was blind to her deeper qualities then. I met her again twenty years later when she found out that I would be lecturing on Christ encounters near her home in Texas. As an adult, I have come to see her with new eyes—as one of those special people endowed with a sweetness and a love that are too easily taken for granted and exploited by the world. It was easy to understand why a person like her would be open to Jesus' presence. Indeed, this experience was her fourth. And one might think that this experience would finally resolve her unusual hardships. But that is not the way it works, it seems. Today, she is battling cancer again, even though her relationships with her family have continued to be loving and fulfilling. Like several of the Christ encounter witnesses, there's been little sustained peace in this 41-year-old woman's life. Even so, she carries the burden of her struggles with dignity and grace.

Once again, as we have seen previously (e.g., K.V.D. in chapter 2), the recipients of Christ encounters do not necessarily enjoy any unusual immunity from painful conditions. Yet, these unfortunate medical and interpersonal crises, rather than standing in the way of a person's unfoldment, can serve to catalyze a search for deeper meaning. For B.S., this search has brought her closer to Jesus. Her graceful acceptance of the conditions of her life clearly stems, at least in part, from her transformative encounters with him. For other people, their search may take them to the threshold of life-changing encounters with angels, gurus, or inner Light—all of which seems to point to the good news of a deeper spiritual nature within ourselves that we can more easily discover when life challenges us to go deeper than ever before.

Like B.S., C.R. was in the midst of emotional turmoil. In this state of vulnerability, she experienced Jesus' presence on several occasions, beginning with a dramatic vision of the crucified Christ. It was as if his own suffering conveyed a full recognition of her pain, and cast her own struggles against the backdrop of his own meaningful ordeal. Once again, her depression seemed to stem from an acute awareness of her own "fallen" state, not from some external, temporary condition. It is a form of depression that is hard to overcome because it is based on a sober perception of her own spiritual condition.

I started having experiences with Christ during the summer of my eighteenth year. Prior to that time I was an atheist. During that season, however, a Catholic friend was helping me find Jesus.

The experiences started one morning. As I awoke, I saw a glowing white hand in front of me with a hole in the palm. The hand moved toward me, and instead of stopping at my face, it went through it and touched me behind my eyes. I immediately experienced a tingling sensation throughout my head and neck, and saw our Messiah in front of me as clearly as one might see a person in the flesh. I saw him bleeding and broken, for I was emotionally the same at that time. When the vision faded, I looked at the carpet where he had stood and saw footprints in the carpet that seemed to glow white. I told my sister and mother about the vision, and they also saw the footprints.

I was going through a great deal of inner turmoil, during my late teens. As time went on, I noticed that Jesus often appeared to me, though not as vividly as during our first encounter. While I feel him often throughout the day now, I usually don't see him clearly unless I am suffering deeply.

At first all this frightened me: I thought I was losing my mind. However, in 1982 when I was thinking these thoughts, an impression came to me, "For you, this is normal," and that comforted me.

From 1975 to 1989 I was severely depressed. I feel that these experiences have helped me enormously in overcoming my depression.

I have seen with my own eyes the infinite compassion of our beautiful Savior, how understanding, wise, and faithful he is to us even when we don't return that love. I have had to struggle with several besetting sins for years, and his willingness to understand and forgive inspires me to emulate him. I learn from his patient example, and what I appreciate most about him is that he is so humble. He never makes one feel as if one were beneath him even though he is Lord of Lords. This was especially important to me during my depression, because I felt so worthless then. (C.R.)

C.R.'s emotional ordeal calls to mind the lives of well-known Christian mystics—like John of the Cross and Teresa of Avila—who, as a rule, underwent periods of extreme hardship, despair, and depression. Sophisticated Christian thinkers have come to see this "dark night of the soul" as a necessary stage in the spiritual journey rather than an embarrassing footnote in the lives of otherwise devout individuals. It is a period in which the seeker comes face-to-face with his fears and recalcitrant nature, and struggles to bring this nature into alignment with God.

In her exhaustive research on Christian mysticism, Evelyn Underhill[3] observes that the dark night of the soul typically begins *not before but after* the mystic's initial illumination. It is as if the bright promise of the initial awakening brings a person's less lofty characteristics into stark relief. The need to understand and integrate the less-than-exalted side of oneself may account for why the Christ encounter does not always eliminate one's struggle in an instant. It may even be that it is the *quality of the struggle*—not its complete resolution—that provides the crucible in which a deeper spiritual awareness, and a more fully integrated personality, can be forged.

5

CONFRONTATION:

THE BEGINNING

OF INITIATION

When Jesus told Peter that Peter would deny him three times before morning came, the disciple was understandably upset and intent on proving him wrong. But when the opportunities arose in which Peter could have affirmed his devotion to Jesus, he acted just as Jesus had predicted. Obviously, Jesus knew his disciple better than Peter knew himself. Why did Jesus feel it necessary to predict Peter's failure? Perhaps because he knew that Peter's fear would undermine his commitment to those he loved and to a spiritual life. By pointing out the problem, Jesus challenged Peter to overcome it.

Throughout the Gospel record, we find that Jesus continually labored to awaken his disciples and followers—and even his enemies—

to their preoccupations, attachments, actions, and behaviors that they placed before their relationship with God. Jesus obviously wanted them to develop beyond their limited understanding and capabilities; and he was willing to challenge them to face the obstacles standing in their way of expressing a deeper love. In this confrontational role, Jesus often orchestrated what might appropriately be called *initiations*— experiences designed to test people, and to elicit a new, deeper response from them. Not surprisingly, many Christ encounters echo this theme of confrontation and initiation. They reveal a Christ figure who brings unfinished business to light so that the witness can eventually resolve it and come into a closer relationship with Jesus or with one's own spiritual nature.

Initiation is often associated with an unpleasant but necessary voyage into an unknown realm or into the underworld itself. From the story of Ulysses' homeward voyage to Perceval's quest for the Holy Grail, the storyline is similar: One must confront and *respond appropriately* to the challenges one encounters in order to prove oneself ready for admission into a higher order, and for full companionship with one's Beloved.

Jesus himself faced numerous tests just before and during his public ministry. Following his baptism, he went into the wilderness where, we are told, he was tested three times by Satan. He was tempted to turn stones into bread, to cast himself down from the top of the temple to prove that God would send his angels to save him, and to assume dominion over the kingdoms of the earth (Matt. 4:1–10). In each case, Jesus defied Satan's temptations. Later in his ministry, he had to confront repeatedly the ignorance of his followers and friends. No matter how much they loved him, they rarely understood the full significance of his life and his teachings. Even on the night of his arrest, while he and his disciples rested in the garden of Gethsemane, his friends could not even stay awake to comfort him in his hour of fear and anguish: He had to face the dread of his ultimate destiny alone. And, finally, when he was given the opportunity to save himself by denying that he was the Son of God, he said nothing to dispel this claim, and was killed for it. Clearly, Jesus remains for us the highest example of an *initiate*: He faced and surpassed the most difficult tests imaginable, remaining devoted in an uncompromising way to his calling.

Few among us would welcome the kind of tests Jesus himself faced. But individuals who have sought to realize their spiritual natures, to live a spiritual life or seek a closer relationship with God sometimes welcome the opportunity to recommit themselves to their path, to overcome whatever stands in the way of their behaving in accordance with their spiritual practice or ultimate relationship with God. Indeed, the practice of initiation has a rich history in the spiritual traditions of both East and West. In the East, stories abound of gurus orchestrating puzzling ordeals designed to deepen their disciples' humility and spiritual understanding. The Tibetan Buddhist guru Marpa, for example, made his eventual successor, Milarepa, build and then tear down a house over and over again. Milarepa found Marpa's angry ambivalence frustrating and utterly puzzling, but he complied with his teacher's directives, nonetheless. He was eventually rewarded when Marpa conferred his teachings and his deep affection upon his obedient disciple.[1]

There are many examples of spiritual initiation in the Old Testament. God commanded Abraham to sacrifice Isaac to see if Abraham would put anything before his allegiance to God. Abraham showed himself willing to obey, and Isaac was spared. In a less obvious situation, one can discern an initiation test unfolding when Joseph is betrayed by his jealous brothers and sold into slavery. He demonstrated the depth of his character not only by the good works he performed in captivity, but also by his eventual forgiveness of his brothers. And in one of the most obvious examples of initiation, Job's lengthy ordeal provides us with a view of a Deity subjecting his servant to seemingly unwarranted tribulations before finally rewarding him for his faith. Through these and other stories, we can see that the God of the Old Testament is a deity who severely tests even those followers who are already giving much of themselves to His service.

In contrast to the Old Testament God, Jesus apparently extended his acceptance and love to his disciples without making them undergo formal trials or initiations. He chose ordinary men without applying any obvious test of their readiness. Having accepted them, he then treated them as fully adequate partners and disseminators of his teachings.

He did not overlook their weaknesses, however, and on several occasions subjected them to the kinds of challenges that resemble initiatory tests. In the most brilliant ways, he awakened his followers and critics to their preconceptions and misperceptions that prevented them from accepting the full mantle of discipleship. And yet, one does not get the sense that he judged them unworthy—only that he could see clearly in them the self-imposed barriers to a closer relationship with God.

For example, when approached by a rich young man Jesus did not turn him away but gave him a choice between following him and retaining his wealth. The young man *chose* to turn away, realizing that his attachments were more important than following Jesus.

> The young man saith unto him, All these things have I kept from my youth up: what lack I yet?
>
> Jesus said unto him, If thou wilt be perfect, go and sell that thou hast, and give to the poor, and thou shalt have treasure in heaven: and come and follow me.
>
> But when the young man heard that saying, he went away sorrowful: for he had great possessions. (Matt. 19:20–22)

Similarly, Jesus did not command the vicious crowd to spare the prostitute from stoning. He simply encouraged them to explore their consciences for evidence of their own sinfulness. Nor did he identify himself to three disciples who witnessed his transfiguration on the

mount: He asked them—as a test of their faith and understanding—
who *they* believed he was.

In some of these reports—which I have termed confrontational
Christ encounters—the process of initiation into a deeper faith, spiritual practice and life begins. The witnesses encounter a situation in
which they discover a personal failing or challenge, but they do not
address it or correct it themselves during the experience. The witnesses
after their experiences are left feeling that they have been *"weighed in
the balances and found wanting."* (Daniel 5:27) They may or may not have
subsequent encounters in which they *do* respond to Christ's challenge
or warning, but these encounters are clearly meant to alert them to the
need to change.

In these accounts, the Christ figure may appear rather stern as he
confronts the witnesses. The emotional effects of this confrontation
can be quite unsettling. Even so, the confrontation points promisingly
to a closer relationship with Jesus and a clearer spiritual path if the
witness can respond appropriately to the spiritual challenge.

In other reports—which I have termed initiation Christ
encounters—the recipients take the process further. Instead of reacting
in an unthinking, habitual way to the challenge, they act appropriately
during the encounter, and resolve the problem before the experience
ends. Once they make this corrective response, their experience typically culminates in a full encounter with Jesus.

Confrontational and initiation Christ encounters are the same
except for how they end. As they unfold, they exhibit the same
apparent two-fold purpose: *to awaken the recipient to an unresolved problem, and to elicit a new response that resolves the problem.*

For some reason, some people are up for the challenge, while
others are not. It might be useful in the future to examine the differences between those individuals who succeed and those who fail in
meeting the tests presented. We might find, for example, that those
who succeed engage in regular prayer or meditation and so are accustomed to surrendering to God's will. Or we might discover that they

are involved in intense interpersonal relationships where they receive regular, honest feedback about themselves and their unresolved issues. Knowing what makes the difference could help us take some steps to increase the likelihood that we will respond appropriately if, and when, we are confronted with such challenges.

CONFRONTATIONAL CHRIST ENCOUNTERS

Many of us, if given the opportunity, would gladly meet Christ face-to-face. But if the following account is any indication of what we might encounter, some of us would be unable to remain in his presence—not so much by his judgment, but because of our own lack of readiness for such proximity.

⤙

My "confrontation" with Christ began with a dream.

I awoke shortly after 1:00 A.M. and sat bolt upright, crying, "No! God, no!" I felt as if I were being forcibly thrust from Christ's presence. A powerful, unforgettable stream of love came from him as I left his presence. I then recalled the entire scene:

I was facing a figure, whom I recognized as my own "higher self" from an encounter in a dream 28 years before. This Being was front and center and to the left of Christ. In the earlier dream, Christ, who was not visible to me, but appeared as a formless dark shadow, asked, "Is this one ready?"

The higher self replied, "No, he is not."

The Christ then asked, "Does he have 'mono-clear-eyed' vision?"

Then I answered, "I know what it is, but have not been practicing." Then, I felt banished from their presence.

Now I again awoke hearing a clear, gentle, authoritative voice asking, "Are you ready?"

Maintaining a singleness of purpose has been difficult for me. My attention span is like a child's. My intentions are solid, but sometimes I do not persevere diligently. However, I still feel the force of the love Christ bestowed on me even as I left his Presence. This memory serves regularly to bring me back to a more focused practice of prayer, meditation, patience, and service.

Except for that beam of love, the encounter was a devastating experience that left me in shock for some time afterward. And to some degree, I still am feeling shaken by it. (W.A.)

W.A.'s failure to develop a steadfast purpose resembles the experiences of the legendary medieval knights whose lifelong quest was to recover the Holy Grail—the cup that Jesus had used for the Last Supper with his disciples.

A few of the knights had managed, after surmounting many difficulties, to find their way into the castle of the Fisher King—the place where the Holy Grail resided. But the few who had been lucky enough to see the Grail had all failed to do the right thing when they initially viewed the Grail, and were summarily dismissed from the castle without knowing what they had done wrong.

The knights' failing was that they had been concerned only with finding the Grail, with accomplishing their goal. They did not search also for the *meaning* of their goal and of accomplishing it. Specifically, they did not acknowledge the importance of Amfortas, the Fisher King. Significantly, Amfortas, too, had failed as a young man to react appropriately in his own encounter with a very mysterious situation:

Years before, Amfortas had been in the woods at night, and had come upon a campfire upon which a salmon was cooking. Tired and hungry, he began to eat some of the fish. There are several versions concerning what happened next, but all the tales agree that he was wounded in the sexual area—either by the salmon burning him or by the owners of the campsite returning and attacking him. Another version has the young Amfortas battling a pagan knight recently returned from the Holy Land, whose lance castrates Amfortas as the pagan knight himself is killed. Regardless of how Amfortas was wounded, all versions agree that his painful wound would not heal.

The Grail seekers had failed to realize that only the Grail could heal the Fisher King's wound, and that their purpose was to make the Grail available to him. They were oblivious to the fact that *finding the Grail was far less important than fulfilling the Grail's purpose*, that is to serve the Fisher King, the wounded soul who without spiritual succor cannot be whole or heal. Like so many of us as we embark on the spiritual path, the Grail knights—upon realizing their ultimate vision of the Grail—became lost in their own blissful experience, and thus failed to ask how the experience might be useful to others.

Eventually, one of the knights, Perceval, managed to pass the final initiation test by doing something so simple that on the surface, it might seem trivial: Perceval asked the question, "Whom does the Grail serve?" He had the presence of mind and heart to look beyond its beauty and to inquire about the Grail's purpose. Perceval thus signified his singular commitment to offer himself as one who would fulfill the Grail's purpose—to heal the Fisher King. By remaining so singularly devoted, Perceval ushered in a glorious new era, when the waters again flowed upon the wasteland, and the Fisher King—who could not heal his own painful wound—was finally healed.[2]

Perceval did not succeed all at once. In the legend, we're told that he had entered the Grail castle once before as a young man but had failed to ask the crucial question. Only after years of heroic effort and maturation did Perceval manage to witness the Grail a second time. Like W.A., Perceval was unprepared for the initial encounter; he was overcome by the light and power of his vision. But he was able to learn from his failure, and eventually become conscious of the "clear-eyed" response that was required of him. We see in the Grail myth a hopeful lesson: In the quest for spiritual understanding, we may need to fail initially, but *initial failure born of ignorance* can give way to eventual success if we have a *conscious understanding* of the goal of our efforts and journey and if we maintain the appropriate, singular aim, that is, if we strive to give ourselves fully in service to a higher calling.

It is probably inevitable that most of us have to go through this initial failure on the way to wholeness. As we take the first steps on the spiritual path, we are initially entranced by the promise of wondrous experiences and greater personal power. We may not admit it to ourselves, but we may still be absorbed in measuring our lives by what we can experience and by what we can attain for ourselves—instead of *by what we can give, and how much we can love*. We run ahead, and leave our human selves and others behind. Our blindness to the deeper purpose of spiritual unfoldment can result in a wounding confrontation for many of us.

My own experience of this painful awakening came about through a dream only days before my twenty-first birthday. It was a coming-of-age dream, and it underscored the fact that I was leaving parts of myself behind in my zeal to experience higher states of consciousness.

I was aware that it was time to reveal my life purpose to my parents. So I went to them and invited them to accompany me outdoors into the yard just prior to daybreak. Bearing no physical resemblance to my actual parents, they nonetheless followed, albeit fearfully and hesitantly. I went outside, raised my arms and began chanting. As I did, lightning flashed across the sky, and built in intensity. Then I lowered my arm and the lightning struck the earth. This repeated over and over again.

My parents grew so afraid that they picked up a lance and threw it into my back. I realized that I was dying as I fell to the ground. They came up to me, and looked down with horror, regret, and fear in their eyes. I said, "I was really your son. But I am the son of the unborn Son, who is still to come."

I realized that they were shocked to realize that they had killed their son, but had not rid themselves of the problem. I had a sense as the dream ended that they would have to deal with a future son of a more profound nature. (G.S.S.#1)

In the dream, I received the same kind of wound that Amfortas received when he bit off more than he could chew. And my words to my parents alluded to a redeemer, like Perceval, who would come later to complete my failed effort. I came to regard this redeemer as a new sense of self that would emerge later in life—as well as Jesus himself, who up to that point had not figured very prominently in my life.

Of course, such lessons are rarely learned all at once. Another dream came on the heels of the above experience, once again to point out my affair with power and waywardness. In this Christ encounter, Jesus exhibits an attitude both loving and stern as he assumes a highly confrontational stance. I was left sobered by its implications.

I dreamed that I was returning from a long journey. I knew that I had been wayward and indulgent during my sojourn. I was carrying a large, ornate, silver cross studded with gems, supporting it against my side, much like a Catholic priest might carry a cross during a procession.

I was walking down a dusty street of a primitive village and turned the corner to see Jesus standing with a group of men. All of them faced me with stern expressions. Jesus said with love and firmness, "I have come to show you what you have built. The only reason I do so is because your Father wants me to, and because I do this so well." As I stood puzzled by this, he hurled a flame-tipped lance toward me. It passed through my sleeve, missing my flesh, and impaling my arm on a stucco wall behind me. Then, he threw another flaming lance, which anchored my other arm.

Immediately, I found myself in another place—in a battle or a gladiator's arena. A large, powerful man in a cloth headdress stood over me. He proceeded to tell me with malicious pleasure how he was going to kill me. Realizing that I must be dreaming, I forced myself awake. (G.S.S.#2)

Years after this dream, I discovered that the lance was highly regarded in the Grail myths. The lance was such an important symbol that a true witnessing or vision of the Grail was believed by many to include a vision of a lance hovering above it. The lance was thought to be the weapon used by the Roman to pierce Christ's side after he had died on the cross. Seen above the Grail, it drips Christ's blood into the Grail. The lance is also the weapon that wounds the Fisher King. Why would such a violent image occupy such a sacred place in these myths? Robert Johnson points out that the lance symbolizes to the medieval mind the incisive, discriminating wisdom needed to get to the heart of what matters most: After all, it was what released Jesus' essence for the benefit of all humanity. As such, says Johnson, the lance is symbolic of the highest expression of masculinity.[3] A measure of the respect afforded the lance survives today in the Greek Orthodox communion mass, where the host, the bread of life representative of Christ's body, is broken by a lance.

In one of the Grail stories, Sir Gawain says to King Arthur, "We have won everything by the lance and lost everything by the sword." Referring to the sword as the primitive, destructive aspect of the male psyche, Gawain's words are relevant to my own dream. I associate the sword with the gladiator who appeared before me in the arena. With his brute power, he is the opposite of Jesus, whose power is lancelike— incisive but not destructive. *In essence, the lance symbolizes Jesus' stance in every confrontational encounter. His attitude is at once wounding, in that he awakens us painfully to our unresolved dilemmas, and healing, in that his love sustains us in resolving whatever remains before us on our journey.*

I came to realize that the warrior in my dream represented, on one hand, my own formidable aggressive and destructive tendencies. I also realized that he symbolized aggressive individuals who would awaken in me a sense of powerlessness—the flip side of the problem. With this realization, I came to see I could become more focused, more incisive and decisive, less wayward, not by suppressing my aggression, but by consciously claiming and constructively using the lance—that is, my assertiveness—and by accepting the challenge of dealing fearlessly with aggressive, critical individuals.

Years later, I had an update on this problem. Jesus was not in the dream; but I clearly felt his influence. I was staying alone during a fishing trip at my log cabin in the Blue Ridge Mountains.

⌒

I awakened around 2:00 A.M. and heard a sound like a rushing wind. Knowing that this sound often foreshadows a dramatic shift in consciousness,* I remained very still and tried to be open. The next thing I knew, I was walking down the stairs to the first floor, fully conscious of being outside of my body.

As I came into view of the living room, I saw a group of men gathered, sitting in a circle near the fireplace. One man, in particular, seemed to be the leader. I knew that he was Pontius Pilate, even though he was dressed in modern casual clothes!

Under Pilate's direction, the men proceeded to conduct a highly confrontational, jeering tribunal of sorts. I was subtly aware that I needed to withstand their scrutiny and to hold to my belief that I was

---

* This sound and pleasant electrical sensation began happening to me in my late teens, and would typically erupt as I would lie down to go to sleep. It usually precedes a lucid dream or out-of-body experience, a white light experience, or the presence of higher beings—especially Jesus. It was a regular experience for several years, and now occurs only rarely. In Buddhism, it is referred to as the "gift waves" of a master. It is called "the conferring of power," and constitutes the "true spiritual initiation."[4] In Mahayana Buddhism, the source is considered to be higher beings—masters who are either incarnate or existing on higher planes of consciousness—who telepathically confer upon the recipient a gift of psychic energy that will stimulate spiritual development.

okay even though they seemed intent on making me doubt everything I believed in.

Eventually, I felt I could not take any more of it. So I willed myself back to my body, and became aware of the bed and the subsiding wind-like noise. (G.S.S.#3)

This experience left me feeling that I had been meaningfully challenged and *tempered* by the men's criticisms so that I would be better able to remain steadfast in the face of judgment and ridicule. Jesus himself told his disciples to expect this treatment as part of the consequences of serving Him: "Remember the word I said unto you, the servant is not greater than his lord. If they have persecutest me, they will also persecutest you." (John 15:20)

Even though I weathered the group's harsh treatment of me for a while, I believe that if I could have withstood more, I would have completed my initiation—and Jesus himself would have appeared to me.

The following account has elements of both a confrontational and an initiation encounter. During the first part of the dream, the dreamer—a 49-year-old art dealer who was in his late twenties at the time—succeeds in overcoming his fear sufficiently to come face-to-face with a Being whom, at first, reveals itself as a great Whale. But later, Jesus himself confronts the dreamer with a problem that he cannot resolve in the course of the dream.

☞

I dreamed that I was on a journey with a group of fellow seekers. There were twelve of us. I recognized several of them as friends and acquaintances. They were all seekers, some mature, some less so. A few seemed advanced and sort of quiet, others a bit more naive and boisterous. There was a sense of excitement and anticipation among them concerning the adventures that we were to undergo on our journey.

We were riding barrels. Each of us straddled a floating barrel as we proceeded along a rocky shoreline with cliffs to the left of us and a vast sea to our right. We sort of hugged the shoreline as it was important to maintain our balance on the floating barrel so we didn't tip over and fall in, and get dashed in the rocks.

I was riding the last barrel in the lineup, and my friend and mentor Herb was the "leader" of the group. He and I were intentionally in the rear of the line to watch over and assist anyone who might have an accident or get into trouble.

Suddenly, there was great commotion and shouting from the others. As they pointed out to sea, two great whales appeared far out on the horizon. There was a sense of excitement and fear, for they could easily swamp us. I was apprehensive and yet I wished, how I wished from the deepest yearnings of my heart, that I could meet what surely must be God's greatest creation—the Great Whale.

Before I completed the thought, the whales knew of my desire and began rushing into shore at a tremendous speed. One stopped and waited, while the other one continued straight toward me. My feelings were mixed. I was terrified and elated at the same time. I tried to remain brave and calm. I was determined not to try to escape, but to face him head-on. Swamped or not, I wished to meet the whale.

At the last second before impact, the whale stopped. Raising its massive head out of the water, it bowed its head before me and softly brushed my right knee. The contact felt sacred. I felt his respect for me and for who I was. I felt deeply, deeply honored. I felt that the encounter was a great gift.

As he swam back to his companion, he turned back, emerging halfway out of the water and transforming himself into a very dapper Jewish male in his mid-thirties who wore a dark blue three-piece suit. The other whale transformed himself similarly. The first man invited us to dinner at his home, high up on the cliff.

The home was beautiful, like a castle. A feast was being prepared outside on the cliff top, and it was a beautiful, sunny day. My fellow guide, Herb, began introducing us to our host, who turned out to be Jesus! In a quiet and shy manner, I hung back, feeling that the others should go first. I just hoped there would be enough time for me to meet him, too, though I was willing to forego the opportunity if need be. I wondered why it seemed easy for the others, and I wished I could have felt more a part of the group.

Herb finally gestured toward me, and said to Jesus, "And now I want you to meet M.R. He goes back all the way to before the beginning, and he has spent many lifetimes serving you and your cause." I was overwhelmed at Herb's introduction.

At this point, Jesus turned and looked at me. He was beautiful. He gazed at me and his eyes penetrated to the depths of my being. He knows everything about me. He knows me as I have never been known before. His look stilled me, and I was not elated or ashamed. I just felt known—absolutely and utterly known.

I knew that just by looking into my eyes, he could tell that what Herb had said was true. He raised his index finger to me and said: "I can see that what you say is true. But you have one problem, and that is you are too romantic. And that makes for confusing considerations."

At this point, I burst into tears. I did not feel in the least bit reprimanded, only incredible love from him and for him. I felt thankful beyond measure.

It has been almost twenty years since I had this dream. In rewriting it, it has just as much impact on me now as it did back then. I can only love this Jesus with my entire being, my whole heart and soul. I feel willing to serve him forever. (M.R.)

Once M.R. actually encounters Jesus, his experience resembles that of a life review, which is a widely reported feature of many near-death experiences. When Jesus looks into M.R.'s eyes, he feels totally known and exposed by Jesus' gaze—and yet, totally accepted, too. Jesus expresses the same unparalleled, discriminating awareness that was symbolized by the lance in my own encounter with him: It's what he does "so well." In M.R.'s case, however, we find that the pain of discovering the unresolved problem is more than offset by the immense love and self-acceptance he experienced in that singular life-changing moment. M.R. seems ready for the life review, while others have found this scrutiny much more difficult to bear. For instance, Dannion Brinkley—who had a near-death experience when he was struck by lightning—was brought before a Being of Light who was accompanied by twelve attendant beings. Together, they ushered him through a review of his life. Brinkley says that he was totally unprepared for the emotional pain of witnessing his own life in review. But years later, when he had a second near-death experience, the work he had done in the meantime—specifically, his efforts to *love* others—made the life review much more tolerable. Brinkley's message to others is *to work on loving those you have not loved;* for that, he says, is the *only* criterion by which he felt evaluated in the presence of the Being of Light.[5]

The following dream encounter is unusual because there is no *direct* confrontation between the Christ figure and the dreamer, only a sense of Jesus grieving about the lack of spiritual commitment from those present. Instead of confronting the witness directly, Jesus appeals to an audience of which the dreamer is presumably not a member. But, in essence, this is really a confrontation.

I would like to share with you two experiences I had in my preteen years.

An unknown boy, who is about my age, and I are shown a map with directions for going to Burma. While looking at the map we have a sense of flying. The next thing we know we are in Burma, with tall grass and elephants, and dirt roads and paths. We turn and walk into a hut. It was a huge room made of adobe-type walls. The boy is no longer with me. I don't see him anywhere. The room is full of people—one can hardly move it is so filled. A big party is going on with drugs, booze, and everybody getting crazy.

I turn to the north wall and see some steps starting to appear. I watch until they are in my full view. Then Elijah and Daniel come down the stairs with Christ following behind them. Elijah and Daniel stop at the bottom of the steps, and Christ stops a few steps behind them.

Christ pleads to the people in the room to follow him, to throw away their worldliness and to follow him.

No one cares; some even laugh and jeer. He keeps pleading but it is no use.

Elijah and Daniel then turn and start back up the steps, ahead of Christ. He takes a few steps, but then he falls to the steps, weeping very deeply. Elijah and Daniel then turn to aid and comfort him. He is weeping because he knows the people are lost.

They do not listen and my heart feels very heavy as I begin weeping, too. Then we (the boy and I) are home again. We turn and look at each other in complete shock.

The whole dream did not have any spoken words to it, even when Christ was talking. I felt and knew what he was saying. I wasn't there as a partaker; even though I was in the crowd, I felt separate from the crowd.

A second, related dream occurred a few months later.

The dream starts with me climbing a very steep mountain. I hear someone calling me, I don't see anyone, but he keeps calling me. I finally look up and there is a light, a very warm light, I can't see his face, but I know it's Christ. He then reaches a hand to me. I can see the marks from the nails. I reach up to take it, but as I do, the rocks go out from under my feet and I fall. It's a long fall, but I experience no fear.

I fall into a river, a very deep and wild river. I can't swim, but I am helped. I don't know how, I just feel the help. I get to shore safely. I start to climb the same mountain again. I get about two-thirds of the way up, then I look up, and at the top of the mountain is a golden cross with brilliant lights showing all around it.

The two dreams more or less started my spiritual journey. (V.O.)

Given V.O.'s youthfulness at the time and the additional threats that have faced adolescents since the late sixties, one can see how these Christ encounters came at a crucial moment in V.O.'s life—perhaps to counteract a possible tendency to give way to the excesses of her generation. While she feels that she is "not a partaker" during the Christ encounter, one can assume that Jesus' intervention was meant as much for her as for the audiences in her dreams—the members of which can be regarded as aspects of herself.

Even if V.O. was not falling short in her commitment *at the time of her experiences,* the dreams were tailor-made to offset any tendencies in that direction. As such, they exerted a *preventive,* and perhaps a corrective, impact on her. In other words, the confrontational Christ encounter may occur to point out past and current waywardness, but also *to arouse a vigilant response in the witness that will counteract future threats to our spiritual unfoldment.*

V.O.'s second dream, though superficially unlike her first one, again points to her struggle to maintain her singular commitment to Christ. The repeated falling away captures the cyclic struggle of many of us. We find that the spiritual journey consists of periodic breakthroughs interspersed with regressions to earlier unresolved issues. The wild river, like the teeming hedonism of her first dream, perhaps underscores the constant tension between the ego's waywardness and the soul's deeper desire to be in union with God, in communication with the larger spirit.

If the problems brought to light by the confrontational encounter are important enough to warrant Jesus' involvement, then our response to them probably exerts a significant impact on our lives. In some instances, our responses could feasibly be a life or death matter. For example, one of my own confrontational Christ encounters hinted strongly that my very life depended on a willingness to do what I was "called to do." Without actually telling me that I might die, Jesus seemed to point out the inevitable—that avoiding my own path might unwittingly undermine my reason for living.

I mentioned this account in the Introduction, but it bears repeating in more detail because it demonstrates just how serious the confrontational Christ encounter can be.

⁀

I am with my friend, Mark, and we are both aware that we are dreaming. We begin flying crisscross patterns through a large new auditorium, as if we are preparing it and consecrating it. We actually pass through each other as we simultaneously pass through the center of the room.

At one point, I see Mark standing in a doorway at the back of the auditorium, talking to someone standing behind the door. I know it is Jesus! Anxiously, I walk through the door and look toward him. At first I am only able to see a bright white light. But then the light abruptly changes into the clear form of the Master.

He looks just as I would expect Jesus to appear, except his hair and beard seem quite dark, and his features sharper. He seems stern, but I feel his love for me. As I stand there, saying nothing, awed by his presence, he asks, "Are you ready to leave the earth, yet?" Startled by the implications of his question, I say, "No." Then he says, "Then go out and do what you know to do." (G.S.S.#4)

Jesus did not have to tell me that I was ambivalent in my commitment; his questioning made it clear to me. At the time, I was considering abandoning some of the goals regarding spiritual work that I had pursued up to that point. And yet, his attitude was so loving that I could feel that he was not judging me. Instead, he intended only to point out lovingly my apparently precarious hold on life due to my failure to heed my own deeper calling to serve him.

I did not say, "Of course I will do it." It took me a long while to come around to that. And yet, in a couple of confrontational Christ encounters, the witnesses responded to Jesus' initial confrontation with a "corrective response" within hours or days of the encounter. By so doing, these witnesses essentially converted a confrontational Christ encounter into an experience of full initiation.

For instance, one 12-year-old girl had a remarkable pair of experiences that together formed a full initiation. In the first, she was confronted with God's wrath. Then, chastened by the overwhelming experience, she remained in a prayerful state for several days afterward and took symbolic measures to cleanse herself. This response then seemed to pave the way for a harmonious subsequent Christ encounter. Writing in midlife about these events, she reports:

☞

When I was around 12 years old, I decided to tease my sister Dorothy. I piled dirt clods on top of our outdoor toilet and waited for her to go to use it. As she emerged, I dropped clods off on her. Trying to elude the clods, she finally broke and ran for the house. I jumped off the toilet and reared back to throw another clod at Dorothy. She ran to the left to escape me. Just as I was about to let go and hit her, I heard a voice. (While it took only two seconds for this to happen, it takes a while to explain the voice and my experience that ensued.)

This voice was like thunder or hearing a great waterfall. The voice sounded like thunder passing through water—like waves. All the voice actually said was, "Drop that." These words were Spirit as they entered me; and they were pure wrath. They washed through me from the top of my head out the soles of my feet. I immediately began to try to open my hand and found I couldn't do it. I struggled several times to open my fingers and couldn't. I felt destruction all around me and realized I could be destroyed on the spot. I recognized this voice as that of God.

Because I trusted God . . . I found myself trusting him regardless of whether I lived or died. As I submitted to him, I felt his words turn to pure mercy. This washed over me again from top to bottom. The mercy seemed to enter my heart like a trickle first. Then like a dam breaking, his Mercy flooded my heart and being. Then, his words turned to pure Love. This washed over me the same as above. This Mercy and Love seemed to run together with the mercy and love I knew, and we were one in Spirit. I felt like I came through it only because I submitted and only because of the mercy of God.

When I submitted and quit trying to open my hand, all of a sudden, I felt like a puppet. My hand opened by his power and the rock fell out. I turned around to see where the voice came from. It had come from the north. I looked and saw nothing. I felt this great sense of redemption, like I'd been purchased at a great price. I then heard Mom calling me.

Later . . . I dreamed that my feet were dirty and I was outside. I heard my phone ringing and I went to answer it. When I did I found myself at a dinner. There were white tables and plates. I sat down and ate two bites (which I believe to mean the two words God spoke to me). Then I asked to help serve and was told, "Yes, but why are you dressed that way? You have to go and change." Then I returned and served the table. I awoke and thought that was an odd dream.

For guidance on the dream, I opened my Bible and it fell to the guest who came to dinner. I then felt a strong urge to wash my feet. They appeared clean, but nonetheless I washed them in a pan of water.

I felt very prayerful for the next four days. I went to bed early one night to pray. Just as my head touched the pillow, I saw clouds in front of my eyes, and an opening came in the clouds. I saw myself standing before an altar with a wooden cross behind it. I closed my eyes thinking this would go away, but then I saw a "man of light" who looked like sunlight. He was in the form of a man. I called him Shiolah, as if I knew him. I also heard a still, quiet voice say, "The Christ."

I then saw a lamb work its way from my heart and run to him. He stood there with his arms outstretched; and this lamb (whom I knew was me) leapt into his arms. He petted and stroked the lamb. The vision went away and then came back. Then the man of light stood by a sheepfold. He set the lamb into a fold at his right side, by his feet. They were in a green pasture and all ate in his light. He was the only light— all else was darkness. The lamb (who was me) ate of the green pasture. The man of light stooped [to pet the lamb]. He straightened and looked at me, there on the bed, and wrath came into his face. Then it left and he held out his arms to me again. (D.B.)

Taken together, D.B.'s experiences move along the spiritual path from thoughtless act and ignorance to confrontation and awakening to corrective response and a sense of Jesus' forgiveness and profound love. Through Christ encounters like hers, we can see the similarities between confrontational and initiation Christ encounters. Both involve a process in which the witness first becomes starkly aware of what stands in the way of a closer relationship with Jesus or a realization of their true spiritual nature or calling. Even though the potential initiate may lack the presence of mind to respond immediately and appropriately to the test, he is often left knowing what he needs to do to continue on a spiritual or life path. By taking corrective action, we can become an initiate in the highest sense of the word—one who is willing to confront and resolve whatever stands in the way of a more complete integration of various parts of ourselves that have been brought to light through the confrontational encounter. Such a frank and honest assessment of our unfinished work prepares us for a more conscious, co-creative relationship with Jesus and other higher beings who are apparently there to assist us in awakening more fully to our own spiritual potential.

6

THE CULMINATION

OF INITIATION

In contrast to confrontational Christ encounters, the initiation encounter ends with the witness responding *during the experience* in a way that removes the obstacle to his own pychological integration and spiritual unfoldment. Like Perceval returning to the Grail castle as a mature knight, these individuals seem to be ready for the encounter.

Some initiation tests in Christ encounters can seem unreasonable to the reader. For instance, the recipient of the following account—a 76-year-old retired nurse who was 61 at the time—was cleaning her home one day and heard a distinct voice issuing from what felt like the "back of her head." The voice asked if she would leave her family and follow him. Clearly, the recipient of the following Christ encounter underwent a most severe test of her faith.

It was a beautiful sunny January morning and I had just finished the household chores in the bedroom. As I started to go into the hallway, I heard a clear, definite voice speak to me. The voice said, "Are you really ready to follow me?" Without question I thought, "I thought I had been following you all of my life." Then the voice said, "If I ask you to leave your husband, children, and everything you know, would you do so?" I was stunned at the question he had asked. Without a shadow of a doubt I was sure it was Jesus who asked the question. So for the next six weeks I prepared myself, my adult children, and my husband for my departure. It wasn't that I loved any of them less; but if I were called, I had to follow him. I described to my loved ones as well as I could what had happened. It felt very final.

When I was finally ready, I was in the same place in the house where I had heard the voice the first time. I said, "Yes, I am ready to follow." Instantly, I knew I would not have to leave my family. It was the Abraham and Isaac story all over again.

Then the voice said, "Get back in the church; you cannot change it from without." Immediately afterward, I sent to northern California for my church membership, and eventually became an elder in the church.

The second thing the voice asked me to do was to make amends with my sister. She and I had never gotten along. So, I began writing her letters, many of which I tore up—but that was the process of getting my anger out in private. Eventually, we made amends and she joined a group I was attending.

The third and final thing the voice said was, "Find Paula and get to know her." Paula was the daughter of my brother who had been killed in the Air Force. She was born two weeks after he was killed. I wrote her a very long letter and made a trip to see her. We stayed up many nights going through old family pictures.

Years later, when I was president of the American Holistic Health Association, I had a very difficult time with several of the board members. I had another vision. I can still see it. It was of Jesus coming down toward me from a small hill with the disciples in the background. He held out his arms with his hands put together and said, "Put it in my hands." I did, and things became better.

I feel he is with me at all times now. (3rd M.M.)

We can see from M.M.'s experience that the Christ encounter can be so compelling that recipients, in their willingness to follow Jesus' guidance, may choose to ignore the wishes and opinions of their family and friends. For those of us on the "outside," who might stand to lose whatever influence we might have previously enjoyed in the person's life, such a turnabout might appear foolish, hurtful, and selfish. We can easily imagine what it might have been like to be one of the wives of the disciples who, we presume, held a much less prominent position in their husband's lives after Jesus called them, and who eventually saw their husbands martyred. And from the standpoint of a potential recipient, we can just as easily fear the consequences of such an encounter. What will Jesus ask us to give up? What will he ask us to do that we've always been afraid to do?

M.M.'s experience, which can be seen as both an initiation and an instructional encounter, suggests that the instructions issued by the Christ figure during an encounter can, themselves, represent an initiation test. For in M.M.'s case, he challenges her to confront and resolve three neglected aspects of her religious and interpersonal life. Such guidance contrasts with the kind of comforting advice that one commonly seeks from other sources of guidance—yes or no answers to already defined questions. Thus we can reasonably conclude that in such Christ encounters an intelligence is operating with an agenda that differs from ordinary humans.

Significantly, Jesus did not tell M.M. that she had to leave her family, he *asked* her if she would. In many Christ encounters, we find Jesus awakening and empowering the recipients through his probing, revealing questions. As we know from the Gospel record, Jesus frequently asked questions as a way to elicit a deeper response from those around him—as if their search into their memories and into their own consciences would stir to life some untapped realization.

In two different Christ encounters—one in a dream and another while meditating—Jesus "merely" asked me questions that resulted in a sense of discovery about myself and deeper truths that I had not acknowledged. Both felt like initiations, however, because the particular answers I arrived at seemed crucial to the furthering of our relationship.

The first encounter happened at about 2:00 A.M. while I was trying to meditate. A group of friends and I had agreed to wake up at that time each night for one month and to meditate for one hour. I had done this once before, and the sense of well-being that prevailed was profound. So I was eager to do it again.

The spirit was willing but the flesh was weak. I was only a few days into the month-long process when I began to find it hard to stay awake for the whole hour.

❧

I was meditating on the sofa beside the bed. I thought that perhaps I could slide down into the sofa just a little bit more and still remain awake enough to continue praying and meditating. As I started to fall asleep, I suddenly heard a sound I'd heard many times before—a sound like a rushing wind. Then I felt Jesus' presence even though, with my eyes remaining closed, I saw nothing but darkness. I experienced the intense energy of his breath upon my face. I felt deeply comforted and loved. Then I heard him ask, "What were you in Rome?" I was puzzled at first, but then a realization came from somewhere within me. I said, "I was two things!" I felt this was a confession of some kind of hypocrisy or deceit. (I had no idea then, or later, what it referred to.) But as soon as I mentally answered him, the energy and sound rose to a new level of intensity. It was hard to bear the intensity of the love emanating from him and coursing through me. I felt that the intensification was his way of lovingly confirming the rightness of my answer. I then lost consciousness and entered a dream that I've since forgotten. (G.S.S.#5)

On another occasion, this time in a dream, Jesus again asked me two questions. I had been working on this book at the time, spending countless hours in front of the computer screen.

☙

I was sitting in front of my computer. Standing behind me were a man and a woman who were involved in a project with me. The computer monitor suddenly opened up like a stage curtain to reveal Jesus from the shoulders up, just a few feet away. A soft purple light surrounded and bathed him. He asked me, "Do you love me?" I said, "Yes." Then he asked, "Do we love Mary?" I was puzzled by this, but said, "Yes." He then said, "Then you are my father and my brother." As the dream ended, Jesus was laughing gently at my inability to comprehend the meaning of his words. (G.S.S.#6)

I have puzzled over the content of these initiation experiences from a variety of angles. Content aside, however, these "mere" questions can be catalysts of the initiation process. By employing this Socratic method, Jesus avoids a parental or teaching role in favor of serving as a transformative agent in the recipient's own inner development. Thomas Moore refers to this kind of relationship as a true *mentoring* relationship in which the mentor is committed to fostering the development of an inner authority rather than serving as a mere substitute for a person's own development:

> A deep father figure . . . settles into the soul to provide a sense
> of authority, the feeling that you are the author of your own
> life, that you are head of the household in your affairs . . . some
> father figures are true mentors, furthering the process of fa-
> therhood by understanding their limited role and by not
> usurping the father's role for themselves.[1]

The following lengthy and richly detailed account reveals how Jesus
apparently works with individuals over a period of time to bring them
to a level of commitment and effectiveness far beyond their previous
experience. The recipient—a Jewish psychotherapist—first experiences a series of awakening Christ encounters in which Jesus intro-
duces himself in a comforting and loving manner. Then, once the
relationship is established, she undergoes an initiation test: Essentially,
Jesus calls on her to go deeper into her spiritual practices, and she
resists. Things get worse as she continues to resist the pressure to
surrender to the process, until she eventually accepts and undertakes
the work she is called to do. The relationship with Jesus is consolidated
through her cooperative response to him, and she goes on to receive
direct guidance from him on a later occasion.

In the interest of preserving the integrity of the account, S.K.'s
multiple encounters are all presented here rather than dividing them
among this chapter and those on awakening and instruction.

⌒

I am 49. Besides working as a psychotherapist, I also do some
writing and have the apparent ability to do healing through laying on
of hands.

I am Jewish, yet am strongly drawn toward the mystical and
metaphysical. It took me about twenty-five years of seeking before I
found a way to integrate Judaism with my other beliefs. Now, after the
experiences I will describe to you, I find myself, once more, struggling
to integrate something new.

Several years ago, I had an experience in which Jesus appeared to me several times during the course of a week. I would be doing something such as going for a walk, and there he would be, looking at me in a loving way. He seemed to be expressing, in a kind, loving, gentle way, "What took you so long?" On a conscious level I wondered what that meant, yet at some deeper level I seemed to understand.

The experience left me feeling protected and safe, and it kindled an interest in Jesus. Being Jewish, I really hadn't learned very much about him.

In looking back at the experience, I am surprised at how casual I was about it. It seemed rather odd but somehow natural. I didn't tell anyone about it at the time.

Three years later, my experience with him was markedly different.

I had been going through a very busy, pressured week. At night I would get into bed quite exhausted. One morning during this time I was awakened by something or someone. It felt as if I had been shaken awake, but not in a very gentle way. It was 4:00 A.M.

I felt compelled to get up and meditate, but I didn't want to. I was too tired, but something wouldn't leave me alone. Almost against my will I got out of bed and went into the other room where I meditate. I really couldn't figure out why in the world I was doing this.

Soon after I was in a meditative state I was aware that to my right side was the presence of Jesus. This time his attitude was much more serious, and I started receiving messages about ways I needed to change. I was to meditate regularly (I'm rather lazy about meditating), do certain exercises first, and make some dietary changes.

The 4:00 A.M. awakenings continued for about a week or two. I was in a very uncomfortable state of mind and body. I was quite frightened. This was not the gentle, benign type of experience I had had with him previously. This was very serious. I felt out of control, as if I didn't have a choice.

My sense of reality was being threatened. How could Jesus appear to me? Why me of all people? Being Jewish made the whole experience even more disturbing. Where was this leading? I wondered if I were going crazy.

The lack of sleep coupled with the emotional stress took its toll. I started having problems with my body: swollen glands, sore throat, a lump under my arm, along with various aches and pains. I was one confused, frightened, unhappy woman.

Finally, I "made a deal" with Jesus that if he would stop awakening me at 4:00 A.M., I would make a commitment to meditate daily. With that, the awakenings stopped, but it took me approximately another month to regain my emotional and physical equilibrium, and I'm still processing the experience, a few years later.

About two weeks into the experience, I suddenly found myself starting to feel sad for no reason that I could consciously identify. The sadness welled up in me and I found myself sobbing uncontrollably. These sobs were so intense they racked my whole body. The feeling that went along with the tears was one of severe grief to have been separated from him for all of this time. The crying continued for a long time and although the feeling of grief was clear I (the "I" that I identify with) couldn't understand what was happening. It was as if a different "me" or part of me was having these experiences and I somehow was not able to fully connect with that part.

The feeling I was left with was that in some way I knew Jesus or was close to him or believed in him at some distant time, and for some reason I was separated from him or perhaps turned away from him.

All of this has led to my working on myself psychologically and spiritually. I have been meditating much more regularly. I'm working at making the dietary changes, reading more spiritual material, and generally working harder at being more loving.

During the time of the "contact," I found myself becoming quite intuitive, and a number of my clients commented on how well the sessions were going. It was surprising to me since I was in such a state of exhaustion. I believe, at that time, I was infused with what I'll call the "Jesus energy." (S.K.)

This account has some possibly unsettling implications. For one, it suggests that Jesus—at least in some cases—does not wait to be invited into our lives but can enter unbidden to impose a relationship and an agenda upon the recipient. While some of us might gladly submit to his will and envy those who have felt his tangible presence, others might feel violated by such an intrusion into their lives.

And yet, Jesus never inflicts pain on S.K. She begins to experience discomfort only as she resists a growing pressure to enter into a more disciplined practice of meditation. It is not as though Jesus makes her anxious or frightened: She becomes that way as she subverts a process of growth that had been intensified by her relationship with him. And then, she feels relieved and empowered when she finally undertakes the prescribed course of action.

People who believe in a Second Coming of Christ have different ideas about how this event will take place. Some believe that Jesus will manifest physically, leaving no doubt whatsoever that he has, indeed, returned. Others believe that the Second Coming will be an internal experience, available only to those who have opened their hearts and minds to him. Even if this question could be answered, there is another, perhaps more difficult question: Will he manifest as the Jesus that walked the earth two thousand years ago or assume a more contemporary form that might go unnoticed by those looking for the biblical figure? One can argue that a person's ability to recognize Jesus in whatever form he appears is a crucial test of one's understanding of his essential teachings. Indeed, having to look beyond the outward appearances of his coming may constitute one of the most fundamental initiation tests of all for those who profess to serve him. Essentially, it is a test that determines if the *form* of Jesus' manifestation is more important than the *Being* clothed by the form.

In the following account, the recipient—a 44-year-old speech pathologist who had the experience when he was 26—encounters a Jesus whose unconventional appearance is presented as a test in itself.

☞

I had a dream in 1972 in which Christ appeared to me. Before the dream began, I had a thought-transference experience. I didn't hear an actual speaking voice, but it "spoke" and said, "This dream is a symbolic message not to be taken literally." The dream then began.

I received the message that Jesus was on a speaking tour of the United States and that he invited me to accompany him for two weeks. I accepted by returning a letter to him. I was subsequently sent to where he would be.

I felt like I was in the wrong place, but something reassured me I was in the right place. I knew that I just needed to look for him. I started wandering around this circus—that's why I didn't think I was in the right place; it was a circus. I soon found a sideshow tent with a sign proclaiming 'Speaking Hourly! Jesus of Galilee! Come see the Savior in Person! Admission Free.' Again this voice came in the dream and reminded me this was all symbolic and not to be taken literally. I went on inside the tent. The tent was empty but there was a stage up front and there was a stagehand there. I explained to him I was supposed to meet with Jesus and that he had invited me. As soon as I said that the stagehand's face brightened up and he said, "Oh, yes! He's expecting you. But the show is about to start so you'll have to wait until afterward." People were coming in, and just then Jesus came around a curtain and saw me just as I saw him. Although I knew it was he, I was surprised at his appearance. Instead of the traditional Christ figure, he was wearing a gray pin-striped suit. He was bald—his face didn't look like the traditional Jesus face. Actually he resembled my uncle Ed. I knew unquestioningly, however, that it was Jesus. He greeted me and apologized for having to rush right into the performance, I guess you'd call it. He gave me a glass of something to drink—lemonade or something.

After a few moments an announcer walked out onstage and said, "The show is about to begin. And now here he is—the one and only—Jesus the Christ." It kind of reminded me of Johnny Carson's introduction. He began to speak. His words to me were like gold, but I don't remember the specifics of what he said. I just remember I was hanging on every word. After a few moments one fellow in the back of the tent said, "Oh, what is this?! I came to see a show not to hear a lot of talk." And Jesus very tactfully replied that he was free to leave at any time. Jesus continued. Several others got up and left, grumbling and muttering. There was obvious skepticism, but some were really impressed. Others showed no doubt. One large fat lady was just beaming as he spoke. Over half had left since he started. Then there was a question-and-answer session, and other people left. Details are vague, but I know that I accompanied him for what seemed like two weeks.

He didn't always say the same thing. He seemed to tailor what he was saying to the needs of the particular people. Over the course of the two-week period, I noticed that the fat lady was frequently there in the front row. I also began to notice another man—it was hard not to notice him—who had bright red hair and wore a loud plaid jacket and orange pants. He seemed to appear quite frequently. I was concerned that he might be some evil or satanic influence. Finally I said to Jesus, "Master, who is that man?" He replied, "You know—but not at this time," and just smiled. Finally I asked him why he looked so different. He said, "Of course, everyone would come to see me if I descended from the clouds in a white robe with angels attending; but that is not my purpose. I'm here to separate the wheat from the chaff. Those who truly know me will recognize me in Spirit—the rest will not know me. In this way I am gathering my true followers." Again I was told by the voice in the dream that the setting of the dream was symbolic—not to be taken literally. (S.P.)

It is interesting to note that the two figures other than the dreamer who remain committed to Jesus have physically undesirable qualities—obesity and tasteless dress—upon which a shallower individual might have rejected them. They, too, contrast with the "ideal" follower even as the Jesus in the dream contrasts with the "ideal" Jesus-like figure. The whole thrust of the experience seems designed both to *test* the dreamer's ability to look beyond superficial appearances, as well as *to give him further reason* to suspend judgment on the basis of appearances. Thus, we can see that initiation goes beyond the mere assessment of the recipient. *It facilitates, as well, a strengthening of the very capacity it is designed to measure.*

The capacity to see the divine behind the lowliest of appearances is one that is highly regarded in the sacred traditions of the East and West. When Milarepa went to meet his guru, Marpa, for the first time, he found him plowing a field.[2] Marpa was dirty and sweaty, and Milarepa did not recognize who he was. Milarepa asked him where he could find the famous guru. Marpa told him that he would tell him after Milarepa helped him plow the field. So began a series of initiation encounters in which Marpa continually frustrated Milarepa's expectations. Marpa would often act selfishly and brutishly as though he was far from the enlightened being Milarepa thought he was. He was obviously frustrating Milarepa's superficial notions that higher consciousness always presents itself in easy-to-recognize ways.

Perceval, too, was tested by lowly appearances. After he had killed the dreaded red knight, and was being hailed as the greatest knight in all of England, he was confronted by an ugly woman who rode a donkey into the banquet hall as his friends were celebrating his amazing feat of courage. This "hideous damsel" confronted him, pointing out all of the work that was yet to be done. Perceval could have dismissed her as a crazy woman, but to his credit, he perceived the truth in her words and quickly called the celebration to a close. He thus passed an important initiation test in his quest for the Grail.[3]

S.P. had no trouble seeing Jesus behind his ordinary appearance. But what happens when we are faced with an *extraordinary* image that holds a great deal of allure but which may ultimately be "less than the best"? Years ago, I had the occasion to tell my friend and mentor, Dr. Herbert Puryear, about a series of UFO dreams that I had been experiencing. They were full of Light and promise, and I was rather pleased with them. However, he asked, "Why do you settle for that?" I became irritated, a sure sign he was on to something. I discovered in further conversation that he thought I was limiting the experience and that I could elect to encounter Jesus, instead. Although the following Christ encounter dream happened years later, it still points out a problem I was having in allowing the Light to become as personal as it might.

At my father's business, I was looking out the side door toward the business across the street. I saw a UFO hovering about fifteen feet above the ground—brilliant red, flashing on and off. C. was on the ground to the left of it. She said to me, "When are you going to see this for what it really is? You see it in two dimensions. When will you see it in three?" I looked again at the UFO carefully, and then saw Jesus standing between the craft and C. He was dressed in a white robe and a headband. He and I began walking toward each other. We held out our hands to each other and clasped them. I was nearly overwhelmed by his presence, his love. I then began to realize that I was dreaming. I was careful as I looked into his eyes to maintain the highest thoughts, believing that my thoughts had a determining influence on sustaining the contact. He held my gaze with a strong, loving expression. I noticed a similarity between his face and a painting that I'd seen before. As we parted, I went back and found Lynn, whom I told about the experience. I told her about how he looked, and she was able to recall the painting that I was thinking about. I wondered if I could take her back and see Jesus with her. (G.S.S.#7)

It's interesting that C. refers to the UFO as *less* than the three-dimensional, personal manifestation of Jesus. It is common to think otherwise—that God's personhood is merely our human, if not infantile, projection onto an impersonal deity. But not everyone thinks that the abstract is preferable or truer than the personal expressions of the Divine. C. S. Lewis, in particular, speaks eloquently about the value of both:

> This talk of "meeting" is, no doubt, anthropomorphic; as if God and I could be face to face, like two fellow-creatures, when in reality He is above me and within me and below me and all about me. That is why it must be balanced by all manner of metaphysical and theological abstractions. But never, here or anywhere else, let us think that while anthropomorphic images are a concession to our weakness, the abstractions are the literal truth. Both are equally concessions; each singly misleading, and the two together mutually corrective. . . . What soul ever perished for believing that God the Father really has a beard?[4]

It is probably true that most of us are more accustomed to experiencing God in one way or the other—either abstractly or personally. If so, then one initiation that we might each face as we approach the experience of the Divine is that of *seeing the Divine from the other perspective* in order to acknowledge humbly the other half of a paradoxical truth.

A 54-year-old theology professor tells of a Christ encounter that took place during his college years. The Christ encounter actually occurred following a series of preliminary experiences, which seemed to test him and prepare him for the eventual encounter.

☞

This is the account of a unique happening in my life that occurred in 1957 when I was a junior at Howard University.

I had been secretly communing with God in the form of Christ, that is, using an abandoned "Bleeding Heart" portrait of him as a focus for my prayers. I lit a candle and knelt before the portrait in the basement of Cook dormitory. Eventually, the dormitory director discovered me in my secret place and, to my surprise, asked me whether he could join me in prayer. For a while we communed there together. In those days, I was deeply into a form of Christ-mysticism. Christ became my daily object of adoration, and the wind became the Spirit of God against my face.

One day it so happened that I came to commune with God seven times. Although I do not recall the context of every event of communion, it all began with the suggestion of a rather verbose but brilliant young idealist that several of us gather at 6:00 A.M. in front of the library to pray for the state of the world. It was barely light when I got there. No one else came. I was sad, but I prayed anyhow; and just when I was about to leave, a strange wind came upon the leaves on the ground and gathered them around my feet. Perhaps this is not an unusual thing, but, at the time, it seemed that God was saying, "Hello!" I returned to the dorm.

Later that day, my girlfriend and I went to the chapel to pray together, for we had resolved that there would be no sexual relations before marriage; and we shared the challenge to resist the urge together through prayer and mutual confession.

Far into the evening, I was alone in my room when three students, all drinkers, dropped by and asked to come in. I obliged them, but soon they were making fun of what they perceived to be my consistent religiosity. They took my Bible and began tossing it around among themselves. I instinctively reached for it but to no avail, as they taunted me about my religious faith and my overheard verbal witness to the wonder of Christ.

Finally, when left alone, I prayed before I went to sleep.

Sometime around 3 to 4 A.M., I was lying on my right side and opened my eyes. Before me was standing a barefooted person in a long garment, the upper part of whom I could not really see. I intuitively sensed that this was neither an ordinary figure nor an ordinary occurrence, for the figure—which I sensed was male— placed his hand, which seemed unusually larger than any normal adult hand, on my shoulder. Then he gently squeezed my shoulder in his hand three times. I had the distinct feeling that the strength in those hands was so great that even a careless squeeze would have crushed my shoulder completely. Yet I clearly knew I was being told not to despair or discontinue searching for Truth. It was a deeply comforting spiritual experience that I knew was some- how related to the seven encounters with God during the previous day, although I did not think of this until later reflection upon the event.

I have meditated on why I was not able to see the face of the figure, and my thoughts have usually settled upon the idea that I was not spiritually ready to do so.

The next day, when I met my special friend, I discovered some- thing that proved to be an amazing follow-up to the previous night's experience. I could greet her and talk of anything except the experi- ence with Christ. For, when the moment came for me to share the experience with her, I could not speak a word of it, even though I tried. I reached the point of crying and facially giving the impression that I was choking on a bone in my throat. Every attempt to tell her of the experience ended in vain, as we sat upon the steps of one of the out-of-the-way stairways of the library.

She reached out to help me as if I were being strangled at my every renewed effort to testify to her of it. And yet there was an almost immediate release from that constriction once I relented from making such an effort.

Eventually, I was able to testify about the event. I later realized that it was not merely a gesture of comfort but a form of anointing of my soul for a special work on behalf of the advancement of his kingdom on earth. I was eventually to enter the pastoral ministry and departed the little church I served in Arlington, Virginia, only after a memorably successful ministry. I had been called, ultimately, to enter academia (what I tend to call the "Teaching Ministry"). To this day, that experience stands uniquely as the most significant, long-lasting, and confirming of all my experiences with God. (W.B.)

It is significant that in each of the events that he could recall, W.B. faced a challenge and then responded to it with prayer and apparent acceptance. One gets the sense that he could have stopped the initiation process at any point by simply succumbing to ordinary, understandable reactions to the disappointments or trials he faced. We might ask, Did W.B. *earn* the visitation from Jesus, or did he simply remove the barriers that normally prevent a person from experiencing an ever-present, greater reality? The question goes to the heart of how one understands the role of Christ in the initiation process. Is he *active* as a judge and an initiator? Or is he simply standing at the door beckoning—waiting for us to remove what stands in the way?

Given the culmination of W.B.'s initiation process, one can look back on the earlier stages of his struggles and appreciate the meaningfulness of the tests that arose. Indeed, when an encounter with

Jesus follows a series of unpleasant, testing situations, one can retrospectively see the design operating in and through those previously unpleasant, unwanted challenges. The encounter with Christ at the end of a testing process serves to remind us to look upon the difficult tests in our lives as avenues to deeper communion with God rather than "punishments" that befall us for no apparent reason.

7

THE INITIATION

OF THE CHALICE

BEARER: ONE

WOMAN'S JOURNEY

Of the many people who submitted Christ encounters for this book, several of them submitted multiple experiences. As a rule, these individuals had been through a process of gradual unfoldment, or initiation, that took place over many years. Rather than presenting the stories in their entirety, however, I elected to use only portions of the entire accounts, to show better their commonalities and differences. And yet, when I received the testimony of Cheryl H., I decided to make an exception.

While I was still collecting Christ encounters in preparation for writing this book, I spoke at a retreat in Palestine, Texas, sponsored by the Association for Research and Enlightenment. Part of the program focused on my work with Christ encounters. Out of two hundred attendees, several people approached me afterward and offered to share their own Christ encounters for inclusion in the book. Cheryl H. was one of those people.

A couple of months later, I received Cheryl's account. As I read it for the first time, I was astounded by the beauty and profundity of her journey. Her account says so much about the role that angels, spirit guides, Mary, and Jesus assume in the process of helping us realize our spiritual natures. I realized then that I could never break up her story into pieces placed throughout the book. I decided that her story needed to stand on its own—as a compelling testimony of one person's spiritual initiation into a deeper relationship with Jesus, and into a life of serving him.

If we look beyond the specific forms of Cheryl's experiences, we can see a universal path of unfoldment that can assume various forms, depending on a recipient's spiritual and cultural orientation. Regardless of one's beliefs, it is a path that demands the utmost in commitment, but which leaves the recipient feeling more free to love and serve others in a variety of ways.

Except for including some italicized comments that might be helpful in interpreting Cheryl's experiences, the following account is in Cheryl's own words.

The Christ encounters I have experienced have been the guiding light and motivation behind my spiritual journey in life. To date, I have spoken to only a few people about them and have rarely given full details. I discourage anyone from thinking that I am special because of my experiences. In fact, I believe that it is possible for anyone to experience the presence of Christ. It is with this in mind that I provide this testimony.

I have often felt unworthy of my encounters with Christ. I am impatient and have a temper; and I tend to procrastinate and avoid carrying out difficult tasks. So I sometimes wonder, "Why me? . . . I am so imperfect!" I can only remind myself that God uses those of us who are ready and willing to serve. His power supersedes our inadequacies. He gives us what we need to complete our assigned tasks. I have finally learned to accept the gift of these experiences and the role that has been given me.

My encounters with Christ have not occurred in a spiritual vacuum. All my life, I have sought communion with God through prayer and meditation, and have sought to deepen my spiritual life through study and service. I have repeatedly asked to serve him in whatever manner he asks of me, and I have asked to be guided to situations where I can best serve.

I have an unusual religious background. I was baptized Catholic and attended Catholic school until I was 10 years old. Although I found the rituals of Catholicism beautiful, the threat of "burning in hell" for my sins didn't mesh with my idea of a loving God. I received harsh words and treatment from some of the nuns at school and was unhappy there.

When my mother married a Jewish man, I was allowed to attend public school with his children. Out of curiosity, I attended synagogue with my stepfather's children. To find out more about Judaism and other religions, I read every book in the public school library on the subject. After completing my research, I decided that I wanted to convert to Judaism. I did so and lived as an Orthodox Jew for ten years. I even attended a Bais Yaakov (religious school for girls) for one year, but didn't like having to live away from home.

During college, I decided to practice the Jewish faith no longer. I felt that so many "fences" had been placed around God's law that the practice of Orthodox Judaism had become a terrible burden. I realized that following religious doctrines would not, in itself, make me a good person. I began to read the New Testament but did not choose to follow any particular religion. Jesus' message of love and his teachings rang true for me, so I concluded that he was a God-sent prophet, but I still did not believe him to be the Messiah. I learned to meditate during my senior year of college when I was taking a psychology course called

Biofeedback and Self-Regulation Techniques. I started using meditation to relax, to promote self-healing, and to solve problems. Learning meditation was a turning point in my spiritual life. In the fall of 1980, during a meditation, I had a vision in which the gates of heaven opened and I entered the light that was pouring out of the gates. When the vision began, I was in a dark abyss, as if I was free-floating in space. Then, a large ray of light appeared, beaming down toward me. I moved toward the light. As I started to enter the light, I felt something try to stop me. It felt as if something was trying to take control of me. Since I had already accepted the Light, however, it couldn't touch me. I was kneeling in the light and looked up to see the source. It seemed as if the light was coming from a large square, as if a gate had been opened. I realized that this must be the gate of heaven, and the surprise of this realization snapped me out of the meditation.

I asked Cheryl to describe the nature of the experiences that come to her during deep meditation. My concern was that readers who have not had such experiences might mistake them for self-directed reveries, rather than experiences that are perceptually vivid and lifelike and that unfold on their own.

When my Christ encounters—and the other unusual meditation experiences—occur, I have no idea that they are about to happen. Most of the experiences have been surprising, even startling. During these experiences, which are infrequent compared to my more mundane meditation experiences, I am not in control of the events, although I do have some choice in how to respond to the experiences and when to end them. I seem to be out of my body; and I appear to have a body through which the senses function, but it's not a true physical body. During the experience, I am encompassed by such a deep feeling of peace that I am hesitant to return to normal awareness.

After I moved in early 1981, I started taking various classes in an effort to develop my psychic and intuitive abilities. I began to meditate daily, whereas before I was not as regular. Through meditation, I met several spiritual guides and found that I could sense the presence of angels. I was drawn by Spirit to learn hands-on healing, and began serving as a channel for healing. In these classes, I met many Christians who talked about Christ and the Christ consciousness. It made me question if I was wrong in thinking that Jesus was just a prophet. It made me wonder if Jesus was indeed the Messiah.

In a meditative state on December 12, 1981, I was led by a nun to a valley surrounded by hills covered with forests. The summits had outcroppings of rock. The nun pointed to the top of a hill. I looked up and saw a burning cross on its rocky crest. I felt as if this was a beacon—a call to Christianity. I began to accept the idea of Jesus as Christ, but I had trouble accepting virgin birth and vicarious atonement—that is, the belief that Jesus atoned for our sins through his crucifixion and resurrection.

During meditation on January 24, 1982, I met a monk who began writing in Spanish on a parchment scroll. As he wrote, I heard the words in English. (I don't know Spanish.) The first thing he wrote was "P." I heard, "prayer, penitence, patience." I thought this was a directive to practice these spiritual disciplines. I asked him if he could give me any clarification about Jesus. He started to write. When I realized that he was writing about Jesus Christ, I grabbed a pen and paper to write down the English translation I was hearing. He confirmed Jesus to be the Messiah and that he was born of virgin birth. I was instructed to attune myself to Spirit. The following excerpt is from what I wrote down as the translation of his writing:

> Jesus is the Messiah. He is the first Son of God among all of us who are sons and daughters of God. . . . Jesus is the example for us in patterning our lives so that we are spiritually strengthened. . . . Jesus came to this world the first time to demonstrate the path we are to follow in this world. He will come a second time to show us the path into the spiritual kingdom.

He will lead us to God and thus fulfill the purpose for which he was sent as Messiah.

After this experience, I started to attend Lutheran church, but I still didn't understand, or accept, vicarious atonement. Several years later, I joined a group meditation class, and my spiritual encounters began in earnest.

⤳

During a group meditation on October 5, 1986, I saw angels swirling around the center of the meditation circle. The angels were placing a jeweled cross in front of each person. (Other members of the group also saw the angels and the crosses in their meditations.) When a cross was placed in front of me, I stood up and it was my height. There was a large emerald surrounded by diamonds at the center of the cross. I thought the green of the emerald was symbolic of my spiritual growth. I placed my hands on the cross and then realized that I was the cross, but I didn't understand what this meant.

Because I was shown yet another cross, I again sought answers about Christ and vicarious atonement. I would enter meditation and ask that I be given understanding of vicarious atonement. I felt that it was very important for me to accept and believe in it. The answer was given to me within days.

⤳

On October 14, 1986, while I was meditating alone, Mary appeared to me with her hands outstretched, standing on a globe of the world. She was wearing a veil and had a small, thin circlet around her head like a crown. She stretched out a hand to me, and I reached for her hand. Upon touching it, I was at the crucifixion. I was on a distant hillside, looking across a valley to a hill upon which there were three crosses.

The valley and hills were covered with spectators. The sky was growing very dark with clouds.

At the precise moment Christ died, I saw a light flash out from his heart, touching the hearts of each person present. I could sense that each person was totally cleansed of sin as if a new soul had been given to each or placed in a state of grace. I felt sad, because so many immediately rejected the light and took back the darkness into themselves.

Next, I was shown the veil to the Holy of Holies being torn in the temple. It was shredded into strips from top to bottom, and fell to the floor. I was given the realization that there were three veils torn: (1) the veil to the Holy of Holies; (2) the veil between heaven and earth—there was now an open path between them; and (3) the veil that had been blinding man to understanding.

After seeing the effects of the crucifixion for myself, I fully accepted Christ as Messiah and the truth of vicarious atonement. I felt spiritually renewed. For the first time, I understood the expression "born again," for that is how I felt.

On October 19, 1986, during a group meditation, Mary appeared to me, holding a silver chalice on a silver tray. There were also little squares on the tray. Mary gave me one of the squares to eat. It tasted fruity and spicy, and was dense. I thought of this as Communion, but Mary told me it was matrimony—a union with God. Next, I was in front of stairs leading up to an old stone chapel that had no door, just an archway. I went up the stairs, into the chapel. The room was octagonal in shape. I realized I was out of my body, and the realization snapped me back hard. My body felt very heavy. I came out of meditation and opened my eyes to the dark room. There was a cross of light glowing on the wall. We sat in the dark and shared our experiences. I wondered if anyone else could see the cross. All of a sudden, it glowed very brightly. This brilliance enabled many people in the room to see the cross, and they gasped in surprise.

The experience of being in a room full of people who could all see a cross of light confirmed for me, yet again, that my experiences while in meditation were indeed real.

On January 10, 1987, during a group meditation, I went up a spiral staircase. At the top was a chalice carved from diamond. It was filled with what appeared to be water. I heard, "Come. Drink from my cup." Next, I was in a large room filled with angels on either side of an aisle. I walked down the aisle, toward the front of the room where there was a throne of light. I realized I was in the presence of God and fell to my knees with bowed head. I felt a touch upon my head just below the hairline. I felt blessed.

I wondered if I was being called to serve Christ beyond my work as a hands-on healer. Was I to become a minister? I had already been approached by the minister of a New Age Christian church to train as a minister in that church. Was there some other way I was to serve? I decided to let myself be guided by Spirit.

On June 28, 1988, while meditating alone, I experienced flying up through rainbow-colored layers of clouds. Each color represented a distinct dimension of life that was being cleansed. As I emerged from the violet layer, I was met by a group of laughing children. Together, we flew up through a layer of gold clouds and a layer of white. We flew up over a cliff and then overland to a rose arbor where we landed.

Most of the children scattered to look around. Two led me forward to a long canopy of blooming roses on arches.

I went forward, alone, toward an old man who stood at the very end of the rose-covered arches. I stopped before him. He asked me if ministry was what I really wanted. I replied affirmatively. He then used his thumb to make the sign of the cross on my forehead, my hands, my feet, my lips, and over my heart—in that order. Then he said, "Go in peace." I wondered who he was. He looked at me with sad eyes and said, "Don't you know me?" With his words, the illusion of the old man fell away and I realized that he was Christ.

This was my first encounter with Christ. It happened so quickly that I didn't have time to react or respond. I was so startled that I snapped out of meditation suddenly. I felt elation when I realized I was being consecrated as a minister. I felt stunned, and then awed, when I discovered that it was Christ himself who had consecrated me to his service. Afterward, I became nervous and fearful because I didn't really know what was expected of me or what form my ministry was to take. A minister of Christ? Did this mean I was formally to become a minister?

On August 3, 1988, while meditating, I swam up a river to a waterfall. I stood in the waterfall, and it changed colors to cleanse each dimension of my being. I felt a very strong flow of energy enter into my body through my left hand and left foot. It coursed throughout my entire body. I felt someone holding my hands. I "looked" without opening my eyes, and I saw it was Christ holding my hands. Then he was gone, but I heard the words, "You are forgiven."

I felt that a physical healing had taken place. Later, I researched the New Testament and discovered that Christ had healed people by telling them they were forgiven. Also, I realized that my physical condition was caused, in part, by an action of mine that had happened more than three years earlier. I felt very guilty about this event and had worried over whether or not God would forgive me for it. Christ's words to me told me that I had indeed been forgiven.

On March 5, 1989, I experienced going to a meadow where I was met by Samuel, whom I recognized as one of my guides. Samuel was accompanied by an old man in biblical-style clothes who had a staff in his hand. Samuel told me the old man's name was Zadkiel. Zadkiel looked directly into my eyes.

I felt as if he could see everything about me and was somehow judging me. I was extremely nervous and felt embarrassed by what he might discover. Finally, he nodded in acceptance of me. I was then told that I would be trained for ordination into the priesthood of Melchizedek.

Melchizedek was a priest-king who offered bread and wine upon Abraham's victorious return from a battle to rescue Lot and the people of Sodom. Melchizedek is Hebrew for "king of righteousness." The Book of Hebrews refers repeatedly to Jesus as the high priest of the order of Melchizedek, and presents the order of Melchizedek as the priesthood of the new covenant established by Jesus. This priesthood is different from the Levitical priesthood, which operated under the law of the original covenant, and which was hereditary. The priests of Melchizedek are called by God: ". . . and no man taketh this honour unto himself, but he that is called by God, as was Aaron" (Heb. 5:4). The Levitical priests served God in a physical temple, but a priest of the order of Melchizedek is a "minister of the sanctuary, and of the true tabernacle, which the Lord pitched, and not man" (Heb. 8:2).

Years later, in July of 1993, I went to a Catholic retreat for three days of silence, meditation, prayer, and study. I found a book about angels in the library while doing some research on another topic. Zadkiel was listed as the leader of a choir of angels called the Dominions, who represent the power of God. *Zadkiel* means "righteousness of God." Zadkiel is God's angel of justice.

Thus it seemed appropriate that I had been judged by Zadkiel, the angel of justice. It also seemed to be confirmation that I really had been in training for some spiritual purpose since this angel of righteousness found me to be acceptable to train for ordination into the priesthood of the King of Righteousness.

My spiritual training began when I received dictated lessons or lectures, which I wrote down while in a meditative state from August 25 to November 11, 1989. I was told that these lessons were part of my training in discipleship. After each lesson, the speaker would close the lesson like a letter and give his or her name. At one point, I had doubts about the authenticity of these lessons and debated whether or not to continue them. Then I received this lesson from a gentle voice that sounded familiar.

෴

September 16, 1989 (dictated lesson): You must be filled with the Holy Spirit in order for the words to be clearly heard. This is the manner in which John wrote. It is the manner in which Paul spoke. It is the manner in which you are being taught. Divine inspiration manifests in many forms. It is expressed in song, in art, in architecture—in any of the creative works which originate from the heart of the Flame Within. You block it with the mind of ego or with the emotional passions of the body's hormonal system. Center and balance self so that the flow of Spirit may come to you. Be cleansed, be healed, be divinely inspired by the Waters of Life—by the descent of the Holy Spirit. It is a roaring river which purges the soul. It is the gentle flow which brings peace. It is the touch of the hand of God. Do not block this gift which has been given you. You must learn so you can serve in the manner which has been ordained and which you accepted. We prepare you for the tasks at hand. Soon, you will be called upon to fulfill your mission in this life. You must be ready to answer when the horn of Gabriel is blown—when you are called. Practice your meditation, discipline self and forego the self-indulgences of temperament and personality which are the stumbling blocks on your pathway. These traits can be controlled through discipline, and discipline you will need to complete the journey you have begun.

In the Light of the Way,

After the closing, I waited for a signature. Instead, I heard spoken softly, "Don't you recognize me?" I then realized it was Christ, but I couldn't believe it. He responded to my disbelief with, "You doubt me? I AM that I AM." He then proved to me that he was Christ. He showed me the resurrection of Lazarus before closing the lesson. He explained that this miracle was performed to prepare his followers to accept more easily his own eventual resurrection.

After receiving this lesson, I would occasionally hear Christ say, "Take up your cross and follow me." I would hear him say this several times a week at all different times of the day: brushing my teeth, taking a walk, driving my car, eating a meal, talking with a friend, or falling asleep. It could happen at any time. I was afraid that this call to discipleship would mean having to give up a normal life with my husband. I wasn't sure what Christ wanted from me. Finally, in desperation, I met with my minister on November 28, 1989, and was reassured by our discussion. After setting aside fear, I was able to meditate, and eventually understood the actions I was to take. I would be allowed to be a wife and, eventually, a mother. I understood that my ministry would not be done behind a pulpit, but in the everyday walk of life—one on one, as I encountered people who are in need of spiritual help or guidance. Every now and then, I still will hear, "Take

up your cross and follow me." I usually hear it when there is something
I am supposed to do as part of my training or service.

⌒

On February 11, 1990, during meditation, Samuel, my guide, took me
to a chamber that had a small ledge by the door. The rest of the
chamber was a vat that held a red, liquid fire—it reminded me of
molten lava. I was told to jump into the vat, not to be afraid, and that
the liquid fire was there to burn away impurities. I jumped. The liquid
fire felt like a warm bath with bath oil in it. After a while, I noticed a
long gate, like a canal lock, that led to another chamber. I floated
through it and into the next chamber that was smaller and filled with
orange, liquid fire. I went through several chambers of different colors,
each of which was smaller than the previous one. By the time I reached
the violet chamber, I realized the chambers were built in a clockwise
spiral. In the center of the spiral was the eighth and last chamber. It
contained white fire.

I entered the white fire and a white robe materialized around me. I
felt the Light within me as a white, hot core blazing forth. I was
transported from the chamber to an assembly hall. The hall was very
large and built in the shape of a Maltese cross with a round center
containing an altar on a raised dais. I could hear crystals tinkling or
water splashing as in a fountain, but I didn't see the source of the sound.
I could hear a soft chant from many voices, but I didn't see anyone.

This meditation left me feeling very spiritually cleansed and psychically
clear. I realized that this cleansing was a preparation for another event.
After a short break, I reentered meditation.

⌒

I returned to the hall with an altar. A bright, white star was floating
high above the altar, beaming light down onto it. I was approached by

two people wearing robes with hoods, and they dressed me in a white robe. They gave me a blue sash belt and a violet neck sash with green trim. They placed two green stripes by the edge of the sleeves.

I was told it was time to choose my path and was led forward to the altar. I entered the Light. I saw a set of doors open into a foggy, nebulous hall. I vaguely heard someone say that the hallway is where each must meet and overcome their fears. As I walked along, I realized I was barefoot. I looked down, and I was walking on the scales of a huge dragon. I almost panicked, but realized I should keep walking and not let it bother me. Every time I started to falter, I refocused on the Light, which appeared before me as a white cross of light. Sometimes I had to close my eyes, walking in blindness to ignore my fears, in order to follow the Light. Later, I was offered a cloth bag filled with water. I rejected it, pushing it aside saying I would drink from the chalice. At one point, I was on a narrow path carved into the side of a curving cliff. Farther down the path, I saw a huge eagle sitting on top of the cliff that overlooked my path. I remembered not to fear, and kept walking. The whole time I was walking, I was carrying something, but I am not sure what it was.

Finally, I saw another set of doors that opened before me into the hall with the altar. I entered the hall opposite the doors where I had exited, even though I felt I had traveled a fairly straight line.

There were many presences in the hall—they were all joyous and congratulating me with silent communication. I realized I had been tested. I walked forward to the altar. A crystal chalice was floating above it. It filled with white fire from the star's light. I accepted the white fire in the chalice and felt it being absorbed into me. I heard a voice call me "daughter of God." I then asked that I not choose my own path but rather have divine will indicate the path I should follow in order to do the most good. Samuel and everyone else smiled. I had passed yet another test with my response—surrender to divine will. I saw a white cross form beneath the floating chalice. I was told to follow the path of the white robe and the white cross.

———————

After this meditation, I knew I had successfully passed yet another test, but I did not realize that it would allow me to enter another level of initiation.

~

While in a meditative state on April 13, 1990, I went to a garden and sat by the reflection pool. Samuel, my guide, appeared and told me to put on a robe. I stood up and unseen hands put a robe on me. It was white with one violet and one green stripe around the sleeves near my wrists. It had a blue sash belt. Very intricate silver embroidery was around the edge of the hood. Samuel then hung a silver breastplate, about nine inches square, around my neck. On it was embossed a chalice. He told me that the breastplate would identify me as the Chalice Bearer. He then pulled the hood of the robe up over my head. He placed a staff of living, blossoming wood in my left hand. He gave me a chalice, which looked more like a footed bowl, to hold in my right hand. It was filled with a clear liquid. He told me to drink.

I sipped and it tasted like cold spring water. As I thought this, he told me it was the blood of Christ. The next thing I recall was drifting in a fog, knowing that time had elapsed but having no memory of what else had happened.

I felt very honored to bear the chalice of Christ. I believe this meant I was given the responsibility to help others find their way to a stronger faith and closer relationship with Christ.

Several years later, I received confirmation of this experience. In November of 1993, I attended a Bible lecture where the speaker talked about putting on the armor of God. She quoted a passage from Ephesians 6:14, which mentions "the breastplate of righteousness." This caught my attention because of the silver breastplate I had been given spiritually, and because of the connection with righteousness in the names of Zadkiel and Melchizedek. Using a concordance, I found a passage about "the breastplate of faith and love" in 1 Thessalonians 5:8. There was a chalice on the breastplate in my meditation, and the chalice is a symbol of love and spirituality.

Cheryl's spiritual guide, Samuel, gave her a staff with blossoming flowers. Hebrews 9:4 mentions "Aaron's rod that budded," referring to Numbers 17:8 where Aaron's rod "brought forth buds, and bloomed blossoms, and yielded almonds." This was regarded as a sign that Aaron was, indeed, a chosen priest of God. At the time, Cheryl was unfamiliar with these biblical references or their relationship to her unfolding initiation.

⌒

While meditating alone on August 31, 1990, I became aware of two presences approaching me through the Light. They came and stood to either side of me, informing me they were there to help and guide me. I was told to stretch out my arms in front of me. I did, and a robe was placed across them. It was floor-length with a hood and full, wrist-length sleeves. The edges and hems were trimmed with stripes of blue, green, and violet. I put it on.

I was then told that the two guides were there to help me walk a narrow bridge without falling. I was also told that I must learn to be a spiritual warrior.

Samuel, my guide, came forward and told me, "It is time for much to be revealed." He took me to a large opened book on top of a stand. The book had letters of fire. I didn't read the words because I was afraid. He told me it was time to take the name Chalice Bearer to heart. He said it was not yet time to leave the city in which I lived, but I should prepare for it. He said I would know when to go, and I should then look in the book to see where I am to go.

Samuel then told me, "Kneel before the Most High God." I went to my knees and then prostrated myself on the floor facedown with my arms out so that my body was in the shape of a cross. There was a brilliant light, and out of its midst walked Christ. I was told to drink from his cup or die. This time his cup did not hold water but rather the blood of his sacrifice. I felt as if I had myself caught the blood from his side in the chalice. I felt myself crying over the love of his sacrifice. My tears washed his feet and I used my hair to dry the tears.

Christ told me he had placed his seal upon me—that I am marked as his. I am to serve with all I am: body, mind, heart, and soul. He told me I would have help, but I must walk the valley of tears. I would see many fall, but as long as I did not stray from the path, I would remain untouched. I told him I was afraid of the darkness of the coming night. He replied that I would see the full glory of his dawn if I did not fail.

The "seal of righteousness" is mentioned in Romans 4:11. "Seal" is also mentioned in Ephesians 1:13 as "sealed with the promised holy Spirit" and, again, in 2 Corinthians 1:22, as "He has put his seal upon us and given the Spirit in our hearts." Cheryl's gesture of drying Jesus' feet with her hair resembles two New Testament passages where women dried Jesus' feet with their hair: Mary Magdalene anointed his feet with oil and dried them with her hair (John 12:3), and a penitent woman washed Jesus' feet with tears (Luke 7:37– 38).

The next few years, I had no meditations that were directly connected with Christ encounters or initiation. Some were very special to me spiritually, but I don't mention them here because they are not pertinent.

My frequency of meditation dwindled during my pregnancy in 1991–92. After the birth of my child, I ceased meditating altogether. I was very tired and worn down. I was nursing my son every two hours around the clock, so I was not getting enough sleep. When he developed chronic ear infections, I became very stressed and nervous. My son slept fitfully and would awaken screaming. Finally, his pediatrician decided he needed pressure equalization tubes. My son had the surgery in June of 1993. In July of 1993, I discontinued nursing when he had his first birthday.

I felt spiritually empty due to my long absence from meditation and communion with Christ. It was time to return to my spiritual work. Leaving my son in the care of my husband, I went to a Catholic retreat center for three days of silence, prayer, and meditation. I sought to renew myself spiritually.

☙

On July 23, 1993, while alone, I entered into meditation asking Christ for guidance in what my next steps were to be on the spiritual path. I saw an altar covered with a white cloth. On the cloth, there was a long "scarf" of the same material, but it had embroidered trim along one edge. It was white on white. It reminded me of the Jewish prayer shawl. I heard Christ say, "There is my mantle. Take it up." The mantle lifted up on its own and draped around my neck, hanging down from my shoulders in front.

I went to the retreat library and researched the mantle in a Catholic book on religious symbols. It is called a stole and is worn by priests at Mass and sacraments. It is the garment of immortality. A white stole is symbolic of confirmation, marriage, and the Eucharist.

The Bible contains several references to mantle, which might help to explain what Christ wanted Cheryl to do. In 1 Kings 19:19–21, Elijah placed his mantle around Elisha as a sign that Elisha was to follow him and minister to him. When Elijah was taken up in the chariot of fire, Elisha took up his mantle, and the spirit of Elijah rested upon Elisha (2 Kings 2:13–15). Since Christ told Cheryl to take up his mantle, it suggests that she would soon be called to return actively to his service, and that his spirit would rest with her to guide her and to enable her to serve him.

When I was contacted by Scott Sparrow about sharing my Christ encounters with others, I knew this was a service I needed to accept even though I had previously been hesitant about revealing the details of my experiences to others. There will be those, of course, who will doubt the validity of my experiences. Some may even scorn or ridicule me. Even so, it is my sincere hope that my experiences might inspire others to delve more deeply into their own spiritual lives, and to seek a path of service to God and others.

May Christ's Light shine brightly in your hearts.

Cheryl H.

8

SPIRITUAL

INSTRUCTION

Most of us probably never consider the possibility that Jesus himself might be available to guide and instruct us. Thus we remain convinced that we will have to "go it alone," deriving instruction and piecemeal guidance from less lofty sources. In the accounts we examine in this chapter, however, we will see experiential evidence that Jesus may, indeed, provide spiritual instruction to ordinary individuals.

Because these experiences contain directions about how one should live, they are potentially the most controversial in the entire collection of accounts. For, if Jesus tells one person what he or she should do, then his teaching might be taken by others as a relevant message to them too, as if they believe that Jesus would not change his basic teachings from one person to another. Beyond the specifics of his words that are meant for the person alone, his instruction might be taken—rightly or wrongly—as a contemporary revelation of his will for humanity. Because of the potential use to which these accounts can be put, we might do well to consider some of the problems created by these types of reports.

For example, one might well ask, Are we supposed to accept the validity of the purported instruction *without question?* If we don't accept them, why not? On whose authority could we depend to validate or invalidate the directives issued by the Christ figure? Another way to approach this issue is to ask, How can we assess the validity of a Christ encounter outside of the recipient's own subjective feelings? These are difficult questions. The difficulty in addressing them may account for why such experiences are largely ignored by religious authorities today.

Certainly, it would be unwise to reject the authenticity of these experiences merely because they conflict with existing doctrines, or even because they contradict the recipient's own personal beliefs. After all, Jesus himself was always shaking people up. He boldly defied the expectations of his closest followers and offended adherents of virtually every religious and political authority of his day. The guidance he offered was and often still is a ticket to martyrdom. He encouraged people to leave their families and wealth and follow him. In many instances, they suffered unfair persecution and eventual death at the hands of the Romans. We can hardly invalidate contemporary Christ encounters just because they challenge established beliefs and expectations, or ask individuals to carry out difficult tasks.

In fact, the opposite may be closer to the truth: Jesus' two simple and bold commandments—the first to love God, and the second to love one's neighbor as oneself—may forever run somewhat counter to those beliefs that gain easy acceptance. For example, Peter's decision to eat at the "unclean" table of the Roman centurion—an action foreshadowed and encouraged by a dream-vision—brought on a storm of controversy at the time because of its deviation from the Jewish law. Here again, an authentic spiritual initiative went against the grain of conventional sentiment and practice. Even when our "neighbors" are so disagreeable that they make the application of Jesus' second commandment appear unreasonable, he apparently meant for us to apply this rule to all persons in our lives.

The question of validation can also be addressed through methods that have been used to assess the authenticity of New Testament passages. Today, some New Testament scholars rely on the "principle of dissimilarity" to discriminate between the authentic utterances of Jesus and those passages that may have been altered somewhat by the Gospel writers and translators to cushion the impact of Jesus' unpopular pronouncements. To put it simply, these scholars are more likely to confer the stamp of authenticity upon a passage to the extent that it *goes against* the prevalent religious ideas of the time. They figure that the Gospel writers were motivated to fit Jesus' teachings into the Jewish prophecies so that Jesus could be seen as the Messiah. Given this aim, they would not have intentionally undermined Christianity's survival by including passages that challenged the prevailing sentiments or religious beliefs of the day—unless these passages were indeed Jesus' own words. These iconoclastic passages, therefore, are more likely to be authentic utterances that the Gospel writers felt duty-bound to include even though the words would provoke and alienate most of their contemporaries.

From this standpoint, contemporary Christ encounters should not be dismissed outright if they contain nondoctrinal teachings. While it is likely that individuals today more readily accept Jesus' teachings than did his contemporaries, it is nonetheless questionable whether Jesus would fit perfectly into any particular religious system today. After all, very few of Jesus' own words have survived to instruct us; and a great deal of modern-day Christianity has been built upon secondary authorities, as well as upon our own questionable abilities to interpret Jesus' few words. If contemporary Christ encounters are what they appear to be—authentic contacts with the founder of Christianity—then Christ encounters should be considered as possibly to contain information that could supplement or clarify the historical words of Jesus. While this might seem heretical, it is a short logical leap to conclude that authentic encounters with Christ might include information that was left out of the final compilation of the brief Gospel record.

KINDS OF INSTRUCTION

This chapter deals specifically with experiences in which Jesus offers general instruction and guidance. One can divide the range of possible instructional material in contemporary Christ encounters into three broad categories based on a comparison with the Gospel record.

- *Identical to the Gospel record.* These utterances are identical, or at least equivalent, to Jesus' own recorded words. They represent an unequivocal restatement or a paraphrasing of his teaching in the Gospels.
- *Contradictory to the Gospel record.* These teachings specifically contradict Jesus' historical teachings.
- *New teachings altogether.* They introduce topics never specifically addressed in the Gospel record, and neither agree with nor contradict his known teachings.

Regarding the first two categories of instructional material, it seems relatively easy to validate or invalidate a particular Christ encounter on the basis of comparisons that can be made with the Gospels. The third category—that of new teachings—is more difficult to evaluate and validate. In the absence of any absolute guidelines, we must make personal judgments. We could start by comparing a new teaching with Jesus' teachings in the New Testament to see if the two seem to reflect the same authorship—a quality that can only be assessed subjectively. Beyond that, we could examine the history of Christianity to see if the teaching ever gained a following among well-respected Christians, and why it was ultimately rejected by the church. Those who accept the validity of other religions can compare the teaching with the tenets of Buddhism, Hinduism, or another great world religion.

We are left, in the final analysis, having to make a personal decision. For, no one who believes that Jesus still lives can say—without demonstrating the utmost in presumption and spiritual pride—that Jesus has said all he will ever say to humanity.

In the accounts that follow, Jesus teaches the recipient an important truth that needs to be acknowledged and applied in his or her life. In most cases, Jesus does not address the practical issues that the recipient faces in his everyday life. Instead, he tends to convey instruction of a global nature that the recipient can subsequently apply in a variety of related areas.

In the following account, one woman receives a revelation about the purposefulness of her suffering. At the time she was 27 and had just come through a series of very difficult situations with her health, career, and relationships. But the experience provided instruction to her that wasn't related just to one specific problem but instead was more universal in meaning. Christ taught her about the crucifixion and how it relates to her life. By referring to his own tragic death as "positive," he helped her appreciate the meaningfulness of some of her own struggles. Significantly, Christ does not specifically cite the aspects of her life that correspond to her own "cross," but gives her the opportunity to conduct her own life review and to arrive at her own conclusions.

⌒

I had a visitation from Jesus on March 6, 1987. It was not a dream. I actually saw him standing alongside the bed. He was wearing a white robe and a red sheath draped over his shoulder. He had a beard, a mustache, and long, light brown hair.

Anyway, while Jesus was by my left side, I was lying on my back with my head propped up and my eyes wide open. We looked at each other, and as I gazed into his clear blue eyes, he said: "L——, everything that happened to you, yes, was negative. But, look at it this way."

Jesus extended his left arm out to the side to indicate that I should look in that direction. I turned my head, looked toward his hand, and saw a movie in the air. In the movie, I saw crowds of people along both sides of a road. The crowd in the movie and I (in bed) observed a gentleman walking down the road, dressed in shabby red and white garments. He looked physically weak and exhausted, because he was carrying a wooden cross upon his shoulder and back. Then it dawned on me that I was watching Jesus' own personal story of the very day he changed the world for all mankind.

Right at that moment of understanding, the Jesus alongside my bed asked, "You see what happened to me? Yes," he continued, "it was negative," and his hand reached into the movie. Then, at the very moment he took the cross off his own back from the movie, he said, "But actually, it was positive."

Jesus removed the tiny cross from the movie, turned around, and faced me. However, the cross in Jesus' hand had transformed into a black addition sign, the size of a baseball.

For a few moments, Jesus held the black cross in front of me, and then said, "This cross is positive."

I looked intently at the black positive sign as he continued.

"L——, what happened to you was actually positive."

While I looked at Jesus beside me, I thought about the meaning behind both Jesus' story in the movie and the black cross he held in his hand. My thoughts quickly reviewed all that I had gone through, and I received a complete understanding of why the adverse events had happened to me. Even though I had physically and emotionally suffered, these hardships were actually a spiritual gain. These losses were for my soul's growth here on earth. I thought how fortunate I was to experience these negative situations in this lifetime. I was so thankful that Jesus came to me and grateful for his healing, by answering my questions.

When Jesus knew that I was finished with my interpretation of the "big picture," he took my left hand and held it in his, saying, "Here, I want you to wear *this* Cross." Jesus placed the black cross in my hand.

I definitely knew that Jesus placed the cross in my hand for I felt two sensations. One, I could feel the weight of the cross (his cross), which was unbearably heavy to hold; and secondly, the cross was like a hot iron on my palm. My hand was scorched. I had to fan myself from the burning heat. Jesus vanished.

Exactly one year later to the date, through a dream I was instructed to look at my left hand. I did so. There in the palm of my hand I saw a red raised scar of the sign of the cross. The same cross that Jesus placed in my hand, upon his visitation. When I awoke from my dream that morning, I looked at my hand but there was no scar. However, I did trace the lines from my palm and sure enough, there were two: one horizontal, the other vertical. Today, my palm lines show that there is a cross.

I am greatly honored that Jesus himself came to me. Sometimes I just wonder. There is not a day that goes by that I don't think of his visitation and what it represents in my life. When I look at my hand it reminds me of Jesus walking to Calvary, and what he said to me that very night: "You see what happened to me! Yes, it was negative, but actually it was positive. This Cross *is* positive." (L.B.)

This account perhaps represents spiritual instruction of the deepest kind, for Jesus takes L.B. beyond a superficial assessment of her suffering into a profound new understanding of her life based on its parallels with his suffering and death. He does not offer specific guidance concerning the directions she should take on the basis of the deeper understanding. It is as though the experience is sufficient to awaken in her a response to life that will affect numerous situations.

I experienced this indirect communication in two Christ encounter dreams that were separated by several years. In both, Jesus spoke to me in symbolic terms about my life, much as he did in his enigmatic parables. I use these experiences as touchstones by which I compare my current choices and attitudes.

In one, Jesus spoke to me about the pearl of great price:

⌒

I am in a dark room. The only thing I can see at first is Jesus standing in front of me. He is discussing the pearl of great price, as though it is something I should seek. He is also saying that I must take care not to collect more than one pearl, for then, I would be unable to close the lid of the treasure chest that contains it. I see a treasure chest in my mind's eye that is stuffed with pearls and cannot be closed.

I then see C., my fiancée at the time. I conclude that Jesus is talking about life partners, and that I should settle on one rather than keep my options open. I say to her, "I guess this means we should be married." I take a sip from a wineglass, then give it to her. It is as though we are consecrating our decision. (G.S.S. #8)

In the parable of the pearl of great price, Jesus compares the pearl to the kingdom of heaven. He tells of a merchant who, upon finding the pearl, is willing to sell everything to have it. "Again, the kingdom of heaven is like unto a merchant man, seeking goodly pearls: Who, when he had found one pearl of great price, went and sold all that he had, and bought it"(Matt. 13:45–46).

It was understandable that I interpreted Jesus' instruction to me in a very specific way during the course of the dream. While he was probably referring to my need to commit myself *in general*, I interpreted his words specifically in terms of human relationships. I came to see the experience as a reminder of a strong tendency of mine: to preserve too many options at the expense of becoming singularly committed to anything. From my practice in counseling, I have come to realize that many people, especially men, are afflicted with this chronic ambivalence.

This experience demonstrates how easily we can look for *specific* guidance from an experience that may only be designed to address a *general theme.* No doubt, this is a tendency that many of us have, especially when we're looking for yes or no answers to complex questions. It's easy to see why individuals frequently overlook the broader implications of their Christ encounters in favor of an "answer" that satisfies some temporary need.

In a second dream, Jesus spoke to me again concerning the same general problem, again offering spiritual instruction with a metaphorical solution.

⁂

I am with Jesus and his disciples on top of a high hill. He is washing our feet. I am deeply moved and honored by his gesture. When he comes to me, he speaks to me while he is washing my feet. He says that I have a problem with my breathing. He says that I need to learn to breathe in a deeper, different way. Once I learn this, he says, I will not have to breathe as often. (G.S.S.#9)

Immediately following this dream, I thought Jesus had been referring literally to my physical breathing. But when I had trouble seeing the validity of that advice, I realized that Jesus was probably addressing my need for spiritual "breathing," or deep meditation, since I had fallen down in my regular prayer and meditation practice at the time.

As time went on, the spiritual instruction of this experience seemed even more global, and I began to see a link between the themes of the first and second dreams. Eventually I realized that Jesus had again referred to the same problem: a scattered, unfocused outlook. In the previous dream about the pearl of great price, the lesson was to focus and to make a singular commitment. In the second experience, it was to slow down, to savor my experience with greater depth and quality, and to place less emphasis on quantity. This, I realized, could be applied to breathing, to meditation, to relationships, and to any number of other issues in my life.

Since many Christ encounters involve indirect, symbolic communications, it seems necessary to interpret them in order to understand their relevance to the witnesses' lives. Some people might object to this, feeling that the experience should remain unmolested by such analysis. After all, if Jesus wanted them to be clearer, wouldn't he just put them into our own language rather than couching his expression in mysterious terms?

It is useful to recall the way that Jesus went about his teaching ministry. He used parables and stories that people have struggled to interpret for the last two thousand years. Hardly anyone would say that Jesus was being unneccessarily obscure. Rather, it is clear that he was conveying a truth that could not be put in simpler, more direct ways. He obviously knew that a simpler version would allow people to come up with precipitous solutions to complex problems.

Spiritual teachers have always resisted the tendency in their followers to arrive at answers that fail to honor the depth of the greater truth. Zen Buddhists contemplate koans, which are enigmatic questions that cannot be answered from a merely rational point of view. A full appreciation of some of the Tibetan Buddhist meditation mantras—though they may consist of only a few syllables—may take years of study and meditative work. Indeed, transpersonal theorist Ken Wilber has observed that the *only* way we obtain glimpses of higher states of consciousness is through symbols that announce the presence of higher realities while, at the same time, defying the mind's incessant tendency to reduce them to recognizable lesser truths.[1]

With this in mind, the following account makes perfect sense. A 6-year-old girl had a dream the day before Easter, in which Jesus spoke to her in symbolic terms. One can see how his use of imagery conveyed information about her parents that may have been impossible to communicate through language alone.

⁓

I had my own personal encounter with Christ in a dream at the age of 6, the night before Easter. The dream has stayed with me my whole life and is as real as it was then.

I dreamed that I was in the living room of the house my family lived in then, when Jesus appeared to me. I was so awestruck, and my heart was touched because he had shown up for me. I immediately ran into the kitchen where my father, brother, and my new stepmother were. I told them that Jesus was in the living room, so they followed me back there, but he wasn't there, so they returned to the kitchen. When I turned around, there he was again. I ran back into the kitchen screaming to my family once again, "Jesus is in the living room." They were reluctant to leave the kitchen this time but did so at my insistence. And again, Jesus was nowhere in sight. Again my family made fun of me and this time they seemed really angry with me; they returned to the kitchen again.

When I turned around, there he was again. He lovingly told me that only I could see him, not my family. Then Jesus took me by the hand to the kitchen to show me something. Jesus pointed out to me the Easter eggs that my parents were decorating and getting ready for Easter. My parents were carefully putting poison in the eggs that were to go in my Easter basket for Sunday. I was stunned with what I saw; the sadness was so much that I could hardly breathe. Jesus then told me lovingly that I would be all right; and he instructed me just not to eat the eggs.

The next day was Easter, and my parents did not understand why their little girl would not touch the truly beautiful Easter eggs my mother had made during the night.

This dream helped me so much as I was growing up. My father was very violent and both physically and verbally abusive in the extreme. This dream made me see my parents as the disturbed people they were, and I did not take the harmful things they said about me as truth. So I grew up feeling that there was something inherently wrong with my parents—unlike most abused children, who end up feeling, as the result of habitual abuse, that there is something wrong with them. Though I have needed therapy because of this tormented past, I was able to develop into a healthy adult, psychologically, as a result of my encounter with Jesus.

I feel I was spared years of therapy that would have been otherwise necessary to put back together a shattered personality, if indeed this could have been done at all. The presence of Christ has been with me my whole life. I'm now 45. I feel *so* grateful. (P.L.)

It seems remarkable that P.L. was able to translate the concreteness of the Easter egg imagery into an overall cautious attitude toward whatever her parents subsequently tried to impose upon her. And yet, she was obviously able to remain flexible enough in her interpretation not to reject *everything* that they would give her from that day onward. We can see that even children who receive such instruction seem to know how to interpret and apply Jesus' symbolic communications. It may be that this knowledge is imparted to the recipient during the experience itself.

P.L.'s experience served to prevent her from being hurt as much as she could have been by parents who did not love her. Jesus essentially told her not to rely on them as much as a child would normally do. In contrast, Jesus tells another little girl to reach out to assailants who have nearly beaten her to death. With advice that goes against everything that one might expect, Jesus urges her to appeal to a compassion that has been totally absent in their vicious treatment of her.

When I was 9 years old, I was taken and brutally attacked by three men for several hours. My whole inner being was begging to die in order to escape the physical pain I was experiencing. At one point I was in a semiconscious state and I could hear the men talking about how to dispose of my "dead" body. I could not speak or move to tell them I wasn't dead yet. I felt my body in the process of dying and was glad that I could finally escape the pain.

Then I became aware that I could choose whether I lived or died. When I realized I had a choice, I couldn't make up my mind. I had strong feelings for both life and death. A voice was telling me that time was running out and I had to make a decision soon! Or it would be too late—I would be irreversibly dead.

As I considered never seeing my mommy and daddy again—their grief over my disappearance—their sadness over not having me with them—I chose to live.

After I made my choice I heard a voice telling me to move my body so the men would know that I was still alive. I could not move even a muscle on my own and then Jesus appeared to me standing by my right foot (I was on the ground). He reached down and moved my legs, and one of the men saw me move and took compassion on me. The man wrapped me in a blanket, took me to his dwelling, cleaned me up, and took me home.

I did not see Jesus' face. I just knew who he was. I say he—what I saw was a large, gentle white figure. There were no words—just an atmosphere of deep, deep caring, and a wave of peace filled my body. All my pain and bruises and cuts felt healed.[2]

Jesus knew something about this brutal situation that few people would have considered: that compassion could be aroused in one of the men, no matter how evil he had acted toward the little girl. For most of us, the most difficult aspect of Jesus' example was his acceptance of his enemies and his understanding of their essential goodness in spite of their harsh treatment of him. His words, "Father, forgive them; for they know not what they do" (Luke 23:34), were uttered while he was on the cross and the soldiers were casting lots for his garment. This depth of love is so inconceivable that most of us tend to exempt ourselves from emulating his example. But this incredible love was not a small part of his life, it was in everything he did. And in the preceding account, taken from Morton Kelsey's *Resurrection,* we find this love manifested again, this time saving the life of a little girl who was encouraged to reach out for love in the most unexpected place.

The following two accounts suggest that some instruction may be so subtle, incomprehensible, or inconceivable that it simply cannot be recalled. The recipient—a 65-year-old woman who had the experience when she was 56 years old—was undergoing surgery at the time of the first experience.

Sometime during surgery, I was floating very high in dark blue space. I did not have the physical body I have on earth. I chuckled at how small I was. I was all lit up like a tiny light. I had little arms and hands and could see behind me without turning or looking behind. I was delightfully happy. I then floated over the hospital. The surgery is on the second floor and my room was on the sixth floor or top floor. I looked down into the surgery room just as though the upper floors were not there. I chuckled again at how small everyone was from my vantage point. I knew that was me on the operating table. Then I thought, "Are you sure?" Just by thinking this, I backed up and went sideways where I could see at a better angle. That was me all right. I then went at a rapid rate of speed back to the operating table. I was not concerned with anyone or anything except a glowing golden light in the shape of an arc over my head. . . . I saw the surgeon and can tell you exactly what he was wearing and what he looked like. However, I had no interest again in what was going on, as the upper right portion of the room was replaced with the same dark blue space I had been floating in. In the upper center of the blue space was a tiny white spot or little white light. This light was getting larger and larger. Then I realized it was approaching at a rapid rate of speed, and it took on the shape of a human. From approximately fifteen to eighteen feet away the figure stopped. It was Christ—when I looked into those eyes I had no doubt. Without speaking, he communicated a message. I cried several times, "I don't know how, I don't know how." I tried to get up to go to him but found I was strapped to the table above the waistline by a white two-inch strap. I told him again, "I don't know how." All of a sudden all the anguish and anxiety left and I was filled with peace—then off to the right appeared crystal clear mountaintops that seemed to surround a valley that was glowing with light. From this valley came beautiful music like a whole choir of angels singing a cappella. I continued to hear beautiful classical music right up to the time I woke up in my room the following morning. I immediately told my husband, "I saw God." He replied, "Well, if you say so."

Later, another encounter occurred in a dream. I woke up remembering that Christ spent the whole night talking to me, giving me important information about something I was supposed to do. But when I woke up, I forgot everything he said! I was so distraught that all day long I begged that I please dream of him once more and hear his instructions again so that I could remember them. Well, I awoke the next day with the same exact feeling, and again I had forgotten everything he said. I decided that whatever he said went into my subconscious and perhaps I wasn't ready to hear it yet. I can only add that each time I feel his presence an undescribable feeling comes over me and it is always a warm and loving one. (A.R.)

A.R.'s experience raises a question: Does the instruction we receive in the Christ encounter need to become a fully conscious realization? Or can this guidance operate just as effectively on an unconscious level, motivating us without our full knowledge of its doing so? In other words, if we forget what he tells us, do we lose the benefit of his guidance? We cannot know for sure. Perhaps, no matter how much we remember after such an encounter, we might still not be able to grasp immediately the full implications of his words. We have seen in many other instances how the recipients find themselves pondering the meaning of the Christ encounter for some time before a fuller understanding sets in. If we place exclusive emphasis on conscious understanding, we might miss a great deal as we move too quickly to a final interpretation. It would perhaps be wiser to rely on the capacity of our deeper selves to register and respond to the full meaning of the experience.

Apparently A.R. was told to do something for which she felt unprepared. Again, it is easy to relate to her predicament. Just as many of us are afraid that God would ask us to do something we don't *want* to do, some of us are also afraid that he'll ask us to do something we don't *know how* to do. We can perhaps take heart by remembering just how unwilling and unprepared his own disciples were to follow him—and how so completely they eventually served him.

While most of the preceding accounts are characterized by instruction expressed indirectly through metaphors and symbols, Jesus can also deliver very direct, practical instructions. In the following account, he manifests to C.M., ostensibly to urge her to offer professional help to a minister she doesn't even know.

⁓

I was 21 years old and was living in a room by myself in a private home. One night, I woke up and saw a dim light over in the corner of the room. The light grew larger and brighter. A voice came from the light, calling my name. I couldn't see any person. But I asked, "Who are you, and what do you want?" I was afraid and knew there was nothing in that part of the room to account for the light. Then, in the light I saw the face and form of Jesus. He was wearing a long white robe and his feet were bare, and a few inches off the floor.

He said, "I have work for you to do." He then asked me if I would serve him, and I said, "Yes, Jesus. What do you want me to do?" I felt very honored to be called to serve him. He said for me to call a certain man, who was a minister, and that he would tell me what to do.

I didn't know the man, but I called him the next day and told him that Jesus had told me to call him. He wasn't surprised. He asked me to come over to his church on Saturday morning, which I did. As we talked, he said that Jesus had promised to send the help he had been praying for. When I told him where I worked—in the public relations department of a large publishing company—he knew that I was the one who was sent to do the work. So he instructed me in what he wanted me to do, and I helped him for several weekends. When the job was over, he thanked me and said it had been helpful to many people.

Soon afterward, Jesus appeared to me again in my room and thanked me for my work. While I have heard his voice since then, I have never seen him again in that way. (2nd C.M.)

It is surprising, perhaps, that Jesus manifested to C.M.—not to commission her to start a new movement or to make pronouncements to the public—but to get her to help someone with a project that would benefit many others. One is reminded that the apostles were frequently guided by the risen Christ on very practical issues in the days immediately following Jesus' crucifixion. While it might be easy to believe that he would assist his closest friends, it might be hard to believe that Jesus would manifest himself today in small-scale situations to individuals who are in no position to effect widespread changes in today's complex world.

It is interesting to see Jesus again exhibiting an indirectness and subtlety in the following account of a dream that goes to the heart of the dreamer's own neglected sense of humor about the spiritual path. He had been active in the Methodist church while in high school but had drifted away during his college years. In graduate school, his roommate was a philosophy major, and the two of them had many long discussions concerning religion, God, and related issues. During that time he began to meditate and take spiritual growth very seriously. By his own account, he became overly pious and much too serious. Being religious was important to him, but that seemed to mean giving up fun and frivolous activity. At this time, he had the following dream:

&

I was attending class in a large auditorium on campus. The room had a capacity for a hundred or more students and reminded me of the type of classroom where freshman history was taught. I was sitting in the middle of the room and there were only a few empty seats remaining in class. Class had just begun and the lecturer for the day was God. I was listening intently to everything God was saying (although I remembered nothing later) when I heard the rear door to the auditorium open. I thought to myself, "Who could possibly be coming in late to God's class?" When I turned to look, it was Jesus coming down the aisle toward me with a smile on his face. He took a seat one row behind me and three seats to my left. I was totally amazed that Jesus would be late to class and still be smiling. As he sat down he looked over to me and winked. I turned around quickly and was astounded! I kept saying to myself, "Jesus winked at me! I can't believe it, Jesus actually winked at me!" Then I awoke with an incredible feeling of peace and joy.

As I pondered the meaning of the dream the next morning, I began to realize that being spiritual did not mean maintaining a serious and pious manner, but enjoying the life we are privileged to have while continuing to listen to God's will and practice the lessons he teaches us. The dream was telling me to "lighten up"—even Jesus winks and has a sense of humor. That dream has meant much to me during the past twenty years, and whenever I begin to take my role too seriously, invariably my mind recalls that dream and gently reminds me to "lighten up." (H.C.)

Some readers might find Jesus' humor out of line with the seriousness he exhibits in the New Testament accounts. Since we know so little about how Jesus lived and interacted with his friends, there is no way to know if he joked and laughed a great deal or maintained a serious attitude throughout his life. Hugh Lynn Cayce—late son of psychic Edgar Cayce—had several Christ encounters during his lifetime. And as he told of them in his many lectures on Christ, he often said that Christ typically exhibited a sense of humor when manifesting to him. Similarly, in Betty Eadie's now-famous near-death experience, she, too, experienced Jesus as a humorous, light-hearted Being. "I'll never forget the Lord's sense of humor, which was as delightful and quick as any here—far more so. Nobody could out-do his humor. He is filled with perfect happiness, perfect goodwill."[3]

In support of this view of Jesus, T.W. experienced Jesus appearing to her and playfully mimicking her solitary dance. But after joining with her in play, he silently instructed her on a neglected dimension of her life—spiritual practice.

⸙

I was in a wide open playground with a merry-go-round. It was a sunny day and I was blissfully dancing around, feeling immense love toward everyone and imagining world peace. I sang out, "I love God" at the top of my lungs. It was out of tune, because I couldn't sing, but I didn't care. In my peripheral vision, there was a figure of a man also happily dancing—trying to mimic my movements. This was very amusing to me, but I just kept flailing around doing my own thing. I kicked up my leg and saw his leg and sandal go up from under the edge of a white robe.

I felt a great sense of friendship and love toward this person, but turned to continue dancing by myself and focusing on world peace. Before I could turn, however, he gently grabbed me by my forearms. I found myself looking straight into the glorious, sparkling eyes of Jesus.

He was radiant, joyous, and laughing, and I felt complete love, acceptance, and fun.

Then it slowly dawned on me that this was actually Jesus Christ! I became slightly self-conscious and vaguely realized that I had been singing out of tune and dancing around like an idiot in front of him.

Still smiling and holding my arms, he led me closer to the ground, until we were in almost a meditative position. (T.W.)

It is significant that T.W. had just fallen into a depression after enjoying a long period of relative bliss and joy. The dream came to let her know that she hadn't done anything wrong, but that Jesus himself was leading her to go within and to meditate. About this dream, she said, "He lovingly showed me how I had been out of attunement [singing out of tune] and could find greater attunement by going within [meditating]. He was helping me to find peace within myself first, so that my ideal of world peace and love could be more fully realized."

The following moving account is an emotionally healing instructional encounter that gave the recipient—a 27-year-old woman at the time—the strength she needed to end her marriage.

☞

Around 1979, I was married, had a BFA in art, had worked as an assistant art director in advertising, and had opened a store in a hotel with imports I was bringing in from Hong Kong. I was successful in many ways, but my marriage of six years was failing. I was still spiritually oriented but not particularly "religious." I had been reared in the Catholic religion, but saw no particular importance in Christianity other than good ethical dogma that is on a par with Hinduism or Buddhism. I was going through a period of strife concerning my marriage. I considered my "vow" of marriage very serious but found my current condition intolerable. I felt unsure and guilty about leaving my husband at the time, so opted to try to "ride it out."

One morning I awoke and sat up in bed. My then-husband was still sleeping. The room took on an eerie grayish misty glow. Before me in full form appeared the Lord, Jesus Christ. There was no question for me who this was. He spoke to me in words, but not words—more of a nonverbal but somehow still verbal communication. He told me to be at peace. He told me it was all right to divorce my then-husband. He bestowed tremendous peace on me. We just loved each other. He told me he would see me again before I died. And then he left. Needless to say, I was awed. I did not even consider myself a good or believing Christian at the time.

I remember laughing that no one would even believe this. Shortly thereafter I disclosed this experience to a friend of mine who had been a printer for the Maharishi Yogi for several years. He shared his witnessing of supernatural phenomena at times and put me at ease with my experience.

I did proceed with my divorce about one year later. I discussed my experience with Christ with my family and friends, but usually was met with ridicule or disbelief. (S.L.K.)

It is probably true that when we feel loved, we are most likely to take some risks to grow and change. S.L.K. apparently needed to know that she had tried her best and could, with a clear conscience, move on. Today at 41, she is remarried and has two stepchildren.

Many scripturally committed individuals do not believe in divorce except in cases of adultery—the only exception cited by Jesus. They would find this account hard to accept, unless the husband's adultery could have been established. Advocates of a scripturally consistent position would consider this experience obviously invalid and the

Christ figure a clever embodiment of deceit. Exponents of a more liberal view might argue that Jesus' teachings today would be somewhat different in order to adjust to the context of contemporary values. Yet neither of these positions say anything about what the witness might *contribute to the unfoldment of the experience*. They are focused on the content of the experience, not the witness's own beliefs and biases, which might distort the content somewhat. From this position, one might say that S.L.K. ultimately *inferred* that Christ approved of her divorce, even though he may not have intended to take any stand at all on the matter. She wondered about this herself in her letter to me, for she asked, "Where does subjective and objective meet? All I can say is, 'I know what I know.' "

Ultimately perhaps, one could say that virtually *all* presumed guidance is generated from within as the recipient reviews his or her choices in Jesus' loving presence. If we accept this possibility, then we can see the more controversial guidance as the product of a self-directed inner search that is activated when we are in his loving presence. From this perspective, Christ encounter recipients gain access to answers *as* they come into his presence, *as* a consequence of having risen in their own awareness to a point where the answers naturally proceed from their own inquiry—not so much *from* him in an external sense. While this may seem like splitting hairs, by locating the source of direction *within* the self as well as in Jesus, it accomplishes two things: (1) It keeps us honest so we don't try to divorce ourselves from the guidance we receive; and (2) it keeps us in touch with the possibility that when we come before Jesus, we are meeting in him the fullest expression of our own evolving natures.

The following dream of a 27-year-old man resembles the earlier dream of L.B. about the crucifixion. Again the recipient learns a profound truth about Jesus' death on the cross—that he lives. Interestingly, the man comes to this realization through the agency of a mediator—an angel who explains the significance of what he has witnessed.

⌒

After I fell asleep, the following happened: I was lying in bed. It was morning, so I got up and went to the kitchen and sat down at the table. As I looked out the window, I saw a cross in the garden with Jesus on it. I was really concerned about this and wanted to check to see if it was really him. I was able to look past the window and found myself outside (but not with a physical body). The air seemed to be in waves, as if the air was two thousand years old and sort of liquidy.

I was able to get very close to Jesus and wanted to know if the cross and Jesus were real. I was now right beside him. I could see him suffering terribly and I felt a lot of distress because he was hurting so much. He was dirty with blood, and I could smell spit and sweat—not repulsive, but just that he had been through a lot of abuse.

The problem was that the weight of his body caused his arms to be too stretched—because his hands were nailed to the cross. As he tried to lift his body up to relieve the pain a little, it caused even more pain. It was really difficult.

I then began to inspect him, as though through a microscope. As I went down over his body, I realized he was naked, and how awful that must be for him to be exposed like that—embarrassing. I felt so much shame that I withdrew and found myself back in the kitchen.

As I sat there wondering what I could do to help, to try to stop the suffering, an angel appeared from above. The angel had no form but was beautiful. The angel told me that he/she had been sent by God to tell me that I had been with Jesus when he was on earth as the Apostle Peter, and to show me that what had been said was true—I would be turned upside down, which I was. When I returned right side up, the angel said I would be able to repeat this whenever I wanted, and left.

I began to wonder at this and sat down. I heard a very loud, terrifying scream. I knew that it was over, Jesus had died, and I felt sorrow, guilt, fear. As I thought about these things, the angel reappeared and told me that I shouldn't feel sad and guilty, but rather that I should be glad that Jesus died because by doing so he had gotten rid of sin—sorrow, guilt, fear, doubt. The angel said that I should be happy. The angel left and I got up to go to the kitchen door that leads out to the backyard and garden. As I approached the door I looked out the window.

It really was Jesus! Alive! And really very healthy-looking. He said my name, but it wasn't my current name. It was another name, but I knew it was mine. He was smiling. It was *so* joyful to see him! It was sunny and I heard music, really nice! I felt a lot of joy!

Then I woke up. My whole life changed for the better.

At the time, I had been seeking and praying for several years to know if Jesus and reincarnation were real. (P.H.)

In this profound experience, P.H. is blessed with a direct experience of Jesus' death and resurrection. Not only does he witness the horror and humiliation of Jesus' final hours, but he enjoys the glory of his life resurrected.

As we have observed in other accounts, the appearance of an angel or of a spokesman alongside the Christ figure is by no means uncommon. This presence typically serves as an interpreter or as a "bridge" between the recipient's human frame of reference and the deeper meaning of what is happening.

Because the above account includes a reference to reincarnation, some readers might reject it out of hand on the basis that it conflicts with current Christian teachings. Since we are not in a position to observe what the fruits of this experience might be in the life of the recipient, we really cannot apply the test advocated by Jeremiah and Jesus for evaluating such experiences independent of their doctrinal implications—by their fruits. . . . Even if the reader accepts the possibility of reincarnation, some will balk at the idea that this man was the disciple Peter: It smacks too much of self-inflation. However, one can also argue that being told that one was once Peter can have a *humbling* effect, just as easily. After all, Peter betrayed Jesus on three occasions. And of course we could interpret the meaning as the dreamer was *like* the disciple Peter.

Perhaps the best approach to instructional Christ encounters is to accept that they express profound truths that simply cannot be grasped directly. The various metaphorical dreams cited earlier obviously had little to do with finding pearls, learning to breathe more deeply, or winking more often. Given the obvious metaphorical quality of these experiences, why should one treat the mention of reincarnation any differently? After all, it might be the best way to symbolize a truth that has surfaced in a recurrent fashion in a person's life regardless of how many actual lifetimes he has lived. Also, by accepting the possibility that one was once a disciple of Jesus, one can perhaps take on the mantle of modern discipleship in a more intense and meaningful way, while at the same time avoiding the mistakes that the historical disciples made along the way.

We have seen that Jesus' instruction is usually very simple. In the following dream, he shows the witness that there is no limit to what he can do—with Jesus as his partner.

~

In my dream, I was riding on a tractor that was pulling a large tiller. I noticed that Jesus was driving the tractor. I was next to him on the right fender of the tractor. I was talking to him about my problems and what I was going to do with my life. He looked at me at this time, and before he could speak, the tractor's right tire blew out. Jesus didn't blink an eye.

I was amazed because we were still plowing. Normally, we should have come to a stop. I asked Jesus how this could be. He answered that there wasn't anything we couldn't do together.

I was still amazed and in disbelief when the left tire blew out. Jesus looked at me again and said, "Oh, you of little faith. Have I not told you that we could do anything together?"

We finished plowing the entire field together on two flat tires. (1st M.H.)

This man is a large, powerful individual with a great deal of emotional intensity. The image of the tractor adequately captures the man's own power. The flat tires reflect his up-and-down struggle with alcohol, drugs, and troubled relationships—problems that have afflicted him for many years. Yet, Jesus seems to say, That's all right, we can deal with that, *as long as we do it together.*

This also seems to be the message in another Christ encounter that happened to a friend of mine who for many years has given lectures and taught courses on meditation, prayer, and other aspects of the spiritual life. An architect by training, he is nonetheless the epitome of a lay minister.

He had been invited to speak to a large conference for three consecutive mornings. As so many speakers do from time to time, he failed to pace the presentation of his material to fit the time allotted, and by the third morning, he was out of things to say.

⁓

Things went well on the first morning. My presentation proceeded smoothly, and for the workshop portion, I elected to use a guided reverie in which the participants were led up a mountain path where they would meet the spiritual teacher that each anticipated.

On the second of three mornings, my presentation again flowed smoothly. After I finished, I opened the floor for discussion. During an animated session with lots of questions and dialogue, I found to my horror that I had inadvertently gotten into the material that I'd planned to present the next day. I had presented it *all* and now had nothing more to present during the third morning segment. Since I was away from my resource material, I was completely unequipped to come up with anything new.

On the third morning, immediately upon rising, I took my Bible in hand, praying that I would be offered guidance for the morning. After a period of intense prayer for guidance, I opened the Bible.

That was not to be! I opened the book and stared in disbelief as I found not a single clue about how to organize the third session. I became angry, and I told God about my anger. In effect, I said that this was his show, that he had brought me all the way to California, and this was certainly not the time to leave me helpless.

With that, I took a shower, still fuming with the Almighty because I felt so stranded. While standing there with water streaming over me, all of a sudden I found myself on the mountain path walking excitedly up the mountain to meet my teacher. As I came around a curve, there stood Jesus—close by and as real as any person would appear to me in an ordinary physical experience.

He was radiant. His arms were outstretched; his pearl-gray robe moved softly in the breeze. His eyes were brilliant as he met my gaze. He smiled ever so gently as he said in the most loving tone, "Bring them to me." And then he was gone, and I was abruptly back in the shower.

Overwhelmed by the experience, I shook and I cried and I laughed. Later I thought, "Sure, that's easy for you to say. But how am I to do that?" Slowly, an idea came to me: I could use the same mountain walk reverie again, but give the participants a longer time to experience their own relationship to their teacher.

When I went to the session that morning, I decided to tell them what had happened, and how the solution for the morning had come to me. They were delighted to enter into the process again. The morning went swiftly, and the reverie was very intense. Afterward, there was no question in my mind that virtually every person there experienced "contact" with Christ in whatever form they allowed him to assume. (2nd J.D.)

J.D. receives a brief, intimidating set of instructions. But he not only hears the words, he *tastes firsthand the very thing that he must invite others to experience.* In other words, J.D. knows that Jesus' instructions are realistic, because his own experience is proof of it. Thus, he must have communicated a profound conviction as he led the audience through the reverie for the second time—a conviction that evidently created a context in which new, amazing things were suddenly possible for the participants.

In conclusion, we have seen that some individuals receive spiritual instruction in their Christ encounters that goes far beyond problem solving for normal day-to-day decisions. In these accounts, we can see how Jesus expresses the import of his teaching through metaphor, imagery, and powerful emotional experiences that convey the essence of his teaching. On one hand, we can feel relief that these teachings generally restate the enduring truths already familiar to Christianity and other religious systems, even though these new messages are embedded in a context of imagery and feeling that alludes to subtleties beyond the recipient's conscious understanding. Thus, these Christ encounters offer a meaningful, somewhat mysterious springboard for future choices and actions—a life-organizing focus that neither loses its relevance nor becomes fully understood.

One might have thought that contemporary Christ encounters would reveal a Jesus manifesting himself to individuals for reasons pertaining primarily to the collective needs of humanity. Given the way Jesus allegedly guided the apostles in the days following the crucifixion, one might imagine him sending a contemporary Christ encounter recipient into some form of service to humanity, revealing the true impoverished state of human affairs, or announcing some direction that humankind should take to come into alignment with divine purpose. Such collectively oriented experiences could, presumably, elevate the recipient to the status of a divinely commissioned missionary, if not that of a modern-day prophet. If so, Christ encounters would pose a direct challenge to organized religion.

As the reader has seen, however, these accounts do not say much about prophecy; nor do they reveal previously hidden spiritual truths. These accounts say much more about the personal relationship of those who have encountered him today to Jesus himself and to their own spiritual natures and practices. In almost all of the cases, Jesus seems to manifest himself to communicate above all else the simple fact of his love for the person during a difficult time in his or her life.

Consequently, while Christ encounters may provide little information that specifically addresses God's perspective on the collective concerns of humankind, they do reveal in detail and heartfelt depth the type of deeper connection that one might apparently enjoy with the ultimate source of guidance and instruction available to us.

9

CONFIRMATIONAL

EXPERIENCES

Christ encounters appear to be, most fundamentally, a profound expression of love and acceptance. Each encounter affects and is interpreted by its witness according to his or her individual needs. They seem to have a corrective effect on the witness's life: If a person is ill, the experience may exert a physically healing effect, or at least alleviate pain and suffering in a spiritually healing way. If a person is emotionally distraught, the Christ encounter can eliminate fear, doubt, depression, and other destructive emotions. If the person has avoided resolving an important issue in his or her life, the Christ figure can confront the witness and provide insights and an opportunity to work through the impasse. When the individual needs instruction or guidance, the experience can point the way. In essence, the Christ encounter typically *illuminates* whatever is out of balance and compensates for it. After bringing problems to light, the Christ figure influences and offsets physical, emotional or spiritual conditions that have gone awry, and reestablishes a healthier balance.

Some Christ encounters do occur to people whose lives do not seem to need a corrective intervention. We have already examined one type that seems to come out of the blue—the awakening Christ encounter. In these experiences, Jesus seems to announce his presence as a way to awaken the person to what could become an ongoing relationship with him, or to their potential for a deeper understanding of their spiritual nature and a deeper experience of spiritual life.

Another type—and the topic of this chapter—is represented by those accounts in which Jesus bestows praise or confirmation upon the person. I have termed these accounts confirmational Christ encounters. In these, Jesus' intervention leaves the witnesses feeling reassured and blessed by his love. He seems to manifest principally to praise the person for work already done, or simply to express his approval for the person without direct reference to anything else. These witnesses were not experiencing any apparent problems when Jesus appeared to them, at least that is the impression created by their testimonies. Yet, unless one embraces a rather shallow view of happiness, it is likely that few, if any, of us have fully "arrived" even during times of relative stability and contentment. It may be that the awakening and confirmational encounters address a need that *always* exists—to resolve the problem of our own perceived separateness from God. In contrast to the corrective encounters, many of the awakening and confirmational accounts reveal a Being who is active and immanent in a person's life during the *good* times as well as the bad.

For instance, the following Christ encounter took place as the witness—an artist—was experiencing a deep sense of meaning about her work. As she was feeling the positive emotions about her art, Jesus appeared to her—reinforcing her feelings and her own assessment of her work.

I was busy preparing for a two-person art show that my girlfriend and I had every year. It was April 1983. I always left everything until the last month. Our show opened in May, so every spare minute between working a full-time job was devoted to the show. I started out with two pastel drawings, very light dreamy drawings called "Dream Roads" and "Transcending." My other pieces were sculpture. I never really planned what I was going to do. Ideas seemed to just come to me. . . .

It was while I was working on a sculpture in my studio. I was bent over in front of the north window sawing wood with a handsaw. I felt wonderful. It was then I looked up to the hallway leading into the room. I saw the lower half of a person in leather sandals and the bottom of a white robe that was so white that it wasn't really solid . . . like bright burning white light. I did not see his face. I looked only from the waist down, and only for a few seconds. I knew it was Jesus. I continued my sawing. The message was loud and clear. I was doing what I was meant to do. I felt very happy. (R.N.)

R.N. experienced Jesus' presence as a powerful confirmation of the path she had already taken in her work. But, she went on to admit, while the sculptures made her immensely happy, they were never a commercial success. This suggests that Christ manifested as a confirmation of her state of mind and heart awakened by the chosen course of action. He did not come to guarantee the worldly success of the project itself. To think otherwise might have left her feeling tricked.

Just as Jesus seemed to manifest to R.N. to confirm her elevated mood and sense of direction, the following encounter took place as a young girl gradually entered a state of rapture as she sang her favorite hymn. Her emotional and spiritual openness seemed to establish a context in which she could then turn and see what is perhaps always there—Jesus walking beside her.

⌒

Ever since my sixteenth year I've wanted to share an experience that occurred when I was a high-school sophomore. I have never shared it with anyone except my mother and best friend, lest someone think I was either lying or hallucinating.

On the maternal side of my family I have Cherokee ancestors; on the other, some were Shakers. Both Indians and Shakers believe that psychic gifts come from God, and that these gifts include visions and "Dreaming True."

With such a background, it was fairly easy to accept my psychic gifts—until the day I saw Jesus. Although I knew that it was a true and valid experience, I found it both exalting and unsettling.

I was walking the three miles to the point where I caught the schoolbus in Seddy, Tennessee. Although I can't carry a tune, I was caught up in a sense of at-one-ness with God, and began singing "In the Garden" as I trudged along.

As I came to the part of the song in which it says, "And he walks with me and he talks with me, And he tells me I am his own," I sensed a presence walking beside me, on my right. I was in a kind of altered state of consciousness in that moment, a state of spiritual rapture. I have never since felt so spiritually exalted. As I turned to look, I saw Christ in a three-dimensional form with red-blond hair, blue eyes, and robes of blue. At first I thought he was a "real" person walking beside me.

I was not on any medication and have never hallucinated. The vision was totally impromptu, incited perhaps by the rapture I felt as I sang, off-key, my favorite hymn. (2nd M.H.#1)

Like many of the witnesses of the Christ encounters included herein, M.H. had other encounters in the years that followed. In one memorable "lucid dream"—one in which she was fully aware that she was dreaming—she again met Jesus face-to-face.

Forty years later, I had a lucid dream of Christ that seems as real as any event in my life. Today I remember the dream in as much detail and as vividly as I did upon awakening on the night the dream occurred.

The dream began in black and white, but later turned into vivid color.

It started with my being on the edge of a slippery, slimy riverbank on a pitch-black night. I couldn't see where I was going, so I crawled along on my hands and knees. Every now and then I would slip over the edge of the bank and down its side, but would catch on to a protruding branch or some other projection that I could not see. I seemed to know that if, in the darkness, I slid down the black slimy bank into the equally black river, I would be lost forever.

Then, ahead, I saw a white light. I crawled toward it and came to a brightly lighted clearing. Now, everything was in brilliant color, and beautiful. At the edge of the forest, vividly colored flowers grew. The grass was a bright emerald green.

In the center of the clearing stood a beautiful southern mansion that gleamed like alabaster. I walked up to the door and knocked, then entered. I was now in a circular-shaped foyer with marble floors. To my right was a circular staircase that led to a mezzanine balcony.

On the balcony stood the Christ I had seen in youth, again wearing a blue robe. He was smiling the same sweet tender smile, and held his arms out to welcome me. I felt that I had come home at last.

Remembering the earlier vision and the more recent dream has helped me face three cancer surgeries and four chronic catastrophic illnesses. I shall be in the hospital by the time you receive this for another operation for cancer. (2nd M.H.#2)

M.H.'s lucid dream resembles the kind of perceptually vivid experiences reported by those who presumably gain a glimpse of the afterlife during a near-death experience. The vivid colors and emerald-colored grass are reminiscent of Betty Eadie's magnificent near-death experience described in *Embraced by the Light*. While M.H. was not in any kind of physical trauma during the dream, her struggle with chronic illnesses might have brought on this "preview" of her eventual destiny beyond death. Perhaps the earlier part of the dream—her efforts to avoid falling into the river—symbolized both her struggle to cling to life, as well as her commitment to remain faithfully focused on her eventual destiny—to be with him again.

The following account also has the earmarks of a near-death experience. But the witness was not, as far as she knew, clinically dead—only recovering from an operation.

At the age of 13, following surgery, as I was coming to, I found myself held in the arms of a Being of white light. I remember feeling very safe and at peace. It felt as if I was a baby being cradled. I turned to look up toward the face and recognized it as Jesus. His robe was brilliant white and he had the warmest, loving smile. No words were spoken but I did not want to leave.

As I felt myself being lowered to the bed (and the pain I knew I'd wake up to) I could see and feel his arms and hands placing me back in my body on the hospital bed. I could hear him say that it wasn't time for me to stay yet. I could feel his love and wanted to hang on to that feeling forever.

When I woke up and saw my mother, I was excited and asked her if she had seen him. I was looking toward where I had felt myself come from. I was hoping to still see him, I guess. No one in the ward had seen anything unusual. My parents always explained it as the drugs from surgery, but to this day, I remember the spiritual sight and feel of the experience.

As I read and study, I accept the experience for exactly what it was: a Christ encounter on a plane other than the one on which we live. (S.G.)

S.G.'s experience was one of profound love, joy, and comfort. Her relationship with Christ was the only issue at hand—not her beliefs, not her mission in life, not her good deeds, not her sins, only his love for her. Understandably, this kind of consoling experience leaves many of us focused on Jesus' role as comforter in our lives. But should we seek such consolation? Some think not. In fact, some non-Christian authorities—like American-born guru Da Love-Ananda—criticize conventional Christianity for overemphasizing consolation at the expense of individual responsibility. But it is easy to see why the emphasis on the atoning effect of Jesus' unconditional love resurfaces with perennial predictability: The experience of his presence confirms it.

Even when a confirming experience of his love is immanent, it is not always easy to accept it. In the following account, a young woman experiences a simple but powerfully direct confirmation from Jesus—but only after trying to avoid him.

In the dream I was in a classroom lined with benches around the walls, with blackboards at one end. Jesus was sleeping on a bench at the back of the classroom, and the feeling was one of anticipating his waking—as the fishermen at sea had, to calm the storm.

As he awakened, I walked toward the door. I was afraid he would look at me, and I felt too unworthy, so I hoped he would not. But he turned and looked at me and came toward me. He then gathered me up to hug me. His appearance then changed to the form of an old East Indian man, with graying hair cut very short and a distant twinkle in his eyes. (R.A.)

R.A. reminds us that it is difficult to feel worthy of Jesus' love. If he appeared in our midst today, many of us probably would, as R.A. did, actively avoid him out of our sense of inadequacy. But he did not wait for R.A. to declare herself worthy: he sought her out. He did not permit her feelings to prevent an encounter. What a statement her experience makes about Jesus' willingness to accept us even with all of our flaws!

As we have seen in other Christ encounters in which the witnesses felt unworthy or exhibited some obviously flawed attitude, the process of spiritual unfoldment does not depend entirely on our own conscious readiness or perceived worth. It comes to us on its own terms, pushing us beyond our perceived limitations toward some greater relationship that we might otherwise refrain from accepting. R.A. may have thought of herself as unworthy; but somehow she availed herself of the opportunity of seeing Jesus. It is likely that such individuals are involved in opening themselves to spiritual intervention while, at the same time, persisting in thinking of themselves as unworthy.

Another interesting feature in this dream, which we've noted in other chapters, is the tendency for this Being of love and acceptance to assume different forms depending on the individual. It is easy for the mind to get bogged down trying to figure out why a particular personal form manifests to an individual, why it changes in the course of the encounter, or what form, if any, represents the "very best" one. Perhaps it changes to counteract the witness's understandable tendency to place too much emphasis on its appearance.

Jesus' assertion of his relationship with the dreamer emerges as the single most important aspect of the following Christ encounter. Again, it does not address a problem or resolve a crisis. Instead the experience confirms his love for the person.

☞

Around the summer of 1966, I had a dream about Christ. Although the contents weren't particularly unusual, the effect it had on me was profound, and I'll never forget it.

I was sitting in the balcony of the large auditorium in the grade school I had attended as a child. I was seated where I usually sat as a member of the school choir. I looked down at the stage and saw Christ.

He wore a white toga with his left shoulder bare. There was a large link chain around his neck, and attached to the chain was a hank of dark hair about five or six inches square. The auditorium was crowded, every seat occupied. Suddenly everyone was quiet, like a great hush. Christ then floated upward in a standing position over the heads of the people below. He floated toward the balcony—halfway between those of us in the balcony and those in the audience below. It was very quiet, and then I heard three beautiful tones of music (I recall them well, as they are the first three notes of an American Indian chant about a firefly, and one which we sang in the choir). . . . After the three tones, Christ spoke, "I am yours as you are mine." At that, I was filled with such overwhelming love and joy, I could never fully describe it. The feeling was so strong that I awoke.

I felt this way for about three days, and could hardly eat or sleep. At that time, I didn't understand the feelings because I also felt a sexual love. Until now, I never mentioned that to anyone as it embarrassed me. I realize now that if all dimensions of my being were stimulated by his love, my sexual feelings would be included, as well. (V.B.)

When V.B. shared this moving dream with fellow members of her meditation study group, they thought that the hank of hair around Jesus' neck signified his mastery over, or integration of, his physical nature. His levitation above the crowd would be consistent with this notion, serving as another symbolic statement of the integration of spirit and body. This interpretation is particularly interesting, given V.B.'s experience of intense feelings of love along with sexual feelings during the encounter. Indeed, V.B.'s sexual feelings *combined with the experience of Christ's full acceptance of her* help her to integrate her human nature and spiritual yearnings.

In a vivid waking vision, a woman sees Jesus manifest in the midst of a prayer meeting. Only she can see him, and she wonders why she, of all people, is worthy to see him.

⌒

I was in Tulsa, Oklahoma, at a prayer meeting (in 1973 or 1974), in the living room of a teacher. There were three rows of people in the living room.

Jesus would first appear to me on the fireplace wall. He was very etheric looking, and I could see right through him. On one particular night, we asked for a blessing. I saw him look up and raise his left hand. Then, moving from left to right, he passed his hand over the group. As his hand passed, a tongue of flame appeared on top of everyone's head. The flame appeared in the crown area on the right side of the head. I even felt the flame. Then we started praying for people.

Jesus came down into the center of the group and became as solid and as clear as everyone else that was there. I even saw clearly how his sandals were laced.

He held out his arms to welcome everyone. The look on his face was like a mother looking at her newborn child.

The blue of his eyes was like nothing I'd ever seen. It was like the whole eye was blue. A blue that was bluer than the sky.

I asked him, "Why me? I'm not worthy to be shown you. There are others in this group more worthy than me."

He said, "Why not you?"

I ended the prayer meeting with tears running down my face. (V.H.)

This dramatic account indicates that no matter how vivid Jesus may appear to a person, others may still be unable to perceive his presence. V.H.'s own sense of unimportance tells her that she did not *earn* the experience. Her puzzled questioning reflects this realization. Significantly, Jesus does not say, "But you *did* deserve it," which would have made his manifestation to V.H. a form of reward. He replied as he did to questions in the Gospels. Given what he said, one can conclude that V.H.'s "goodness" or "sinfulness" was not the issue at all. Jesus' love was the issue, and the experience simply confirmed it. His elegant and powerful question essentially challenged her—and anyone else for that matter—to present *anything* about herself that could possibly overshadow his acceptance of her. The question, "Why not you?" was, perhaps, a succinct statement of his radically inclusive spirit, of his acceptance of each and every person he meets.

Christians have often invoked Jesus' presence through ritually enacting significant moments in Jesus' life. From the practice of Holy Communion to the pope's annual retracing of Jesus' final walk, Christians have historically turned to ritual reenactment as a way to increase their sense of Jesus' abiding presence in their lives.

In this vein, many have traveled to the Holy Land and walked the dusty roads that Jesus and his disciples walked two thousand years ago. In the following account, a woman sees Jesus walking toward her on the banks of the river Jordan.

☞

A very special moment with the Master came in 1975 while visiting in the Holy Land.

My husband had a dear Jewish friend who lived in Tel Aviv. He arranged for our lodging and planned tours for us when he and his wife were not free to be with us.

On a tour that took us to the Jordan River, I managed to linger behind the tour group. I sat, or stood—I cannot remember now— by the riverbank. My thoughts were of Jesus and his baptism by John.

Suddenly, I looked up to see the figure of Jesus walking toward me. Today, I cannot remember what I did or said (or if I spoke). He did not speak, but it was more than a "picturing of him." Quietly he faded from my vision. I was filled with a renewal of Spirit. (M.E.#2)

Once again, so much was conveyed and confirmed in a few silent moments of encountering Jesus: his availability, his aliveness, and his love for M.E. About the seeming brevity of such experiences, Teresa of Avila once said that "in an instant the mind learns so many things at once that if the imagination and the intellect spend years striving to enumerate them, they could not recall a thousandth part of them.[1]

If we take St. Teresa's words to heart, then brevity is no measure of the significance of a Christ encounter. In the following account, a woman experiences in a few words the awesome power of Jesus' confirmation of her.

⁓

My vision of Christ came to me in a dream.

I dream quite often about being in a classroom with various teachers, but this time there—standing in front of the class—was Jesus Christ.

He was standing at the blackboard wearing a white robe. His face was not feminine or physically beautiful as he is sometimes depicted, but his face was kind-looking, a slender face with a dark beard and dark eyes.

He had a kind of glow through his skin. Everyone in the class had a great respect and awe for him because he was known by all there to be the greatest teacher.

He spoke to the class using such words as "verily." I can't remember his exact words, but he told us that the destruction of the earth had been averted because people had begun to bring forth spiritual energy and send out visualizations for world healing. Then he turned to me and said, "Linda, you are doing better."

When I woke up I knew that this was not just a dream. It felt like it had been real. I tried to think about how I was doing better, and then I remembered that a couple of days before I realized that the most important thing was for me to be loving and I prayed to be loving. Also, after that, I knew that Jesus is really there and I know that I can call on him, and when I do, he comes to me in visions and is always a healing force in my life. (L.H.)

L.H. welcomes Jesus' approval of her as a great gift and source of information about her progress. By mentioning that she is "doing better," however, Jesus also implies that she is still lacking in some way. So, in this encounter we see the teacher-taskmaster side of Jesus alongside the comforter-consoler. As such, it is an instructional Christ encounter, too. Fully accepting of L.H., he confirms her. Fully knowing her, he also points subtly to work she has yet to do.

Perhaps the ultimate confirmation is to be ushered by Jesus into the realization that we are, as he is, boundless and unlimited beings. The following account was submitted by a 36-year-old woman who, at the time of the experience, was a member of a Christian renunciate and service order. Like many other witnesses in Christ encounters, she has had several mystical encounters with Jesus.

I was meditating in the chapel with the other members of the order. Our collective prayers were to the Master, Jesus, in a spirit of giving ourselves to him as channels of blessing and service. Then I felt the loving Presence with me and saw white Light pouring into my body and radiating from my face. As I meditated upon this Light and Jesus, I was led through an experience like a near-death experience. I passed through a tunnellike passage, into an area of soft blue light; deeper into a dark area and finally into the midst of a brilliant, shining sun. I remained there in this Light like no other and heard his voice different and separate from the still small voice of my intuition. He said only, "Lo, I am with you always, even unto the end."

I was shown and told a lot from a perspective of a higher knowing but don't remember what I was given. What has remained with me is that I experienced myself as a perfect, whole being with no sense of boundaries or limitations. I was in a complete union and peace with God: There was no separation, not even a concept of being separate. Creator and creation were one in a vibration of infinite love. I was overwhelmed by the beauty and love that I experienced for myself and all other people at that moment.

In coming out of the meditation, I remember feeling a sense of grief or loss at not being able to maintain the level of conscious awareness and manifestation of that true Self in my everyday life. It was like feeling the atmosphere change when you come down from the high altitudes of a mountain. I wondered why I could not just be that greater "me" all the time. My personality felt like a burden I was carrying around. But I knew that this was the challenge and purpose of my life now—to manifest that awareness and to see others in that light. (C.N.)

C.N.'s experience of loss as she returned to her "ordinary" state of consciousness underscores one of the dilemmas posed by the Christ encounter: The witness is thereafter consigned to live with the memory of what may never again occur. As Texas-born mystic and author Walter Starcke has said, it's like having a ten-gallon experience and then returning to a one-quart mind.[2]

The confirmational Christ encounter can resemble a parent-child encounter, in which the parent—beyond requiring anything of the child—simply overflows with love and praise toward the child. A woman experienced silent but profound confirmation as she saw Jesus briefly manifest to her while she was driving.

The first time Jesus appeared to me was when I was driving my car through Cranston, a city near Rhode Island's capital. He appeared only briefly. I hesitate to say it was an appearance in the physical sense, but I did *see* him. He was sitting in the passenger seat with the seat belt on! He looked at me but said nothing. The love and peace I felt from him were overpowering. He was looking at me, not with pride, but with pleasure. In other words, he seemed pleased with me and looked at me with the type of love a father would have for his child. (M.W.)

Even though M.W. experienced only love and confirmation from Jesus, she was still left wondering, Why me, and what next? When she told her minister about the encounter, she found him supporting the idea that God was calling her. But to do what? While she admits that she gets scared because she doesn't feel worthy of this attention, she says that she's "more afraid of not doing what God wants me to do." She goes on to say, "It's no exaggeration to say that I am going through probably the most humbling and exhilarating period of my life. I understand now why the Apostles just stopped what they were doing and followed Christ. If he appears to me again and tells me to do whatever, I will do it."

It is understandable that M.W. assumed that Jesus had some specific agenda for her, but with this assumption she runs the risk of overlooking the most obvious implication of her encounter—that he manifested to express his pleasure. There is no evidence that he intended to inaugurate a new course of action. As already suggested, the Christ encounter stimulates a search for greater meaning and new directions. Whether it is his intent that we should be so galvanized that we pursue a dramatic new course in life is by no means clear from many of the confirmational-type encounters.

Through the following encounter, a 52-year-old registered nurse came to realize that Jesus is "*alive now* in the present." P.B.'s experience is a remarkably luminous and cosmic example of a confirmational Christ encounter. In addition to portraying Jesus as a Light Being with a sublimely beautiful human side, it includes, as well, the presence of angelic or "spirit guides" who serve as intermediaries between her and the Christ being.

❦

I dream that I am with my spirit guides, whose names I know to be Altumus and Miraetha. They are teaching me and giving me a progress report. Altumus smiles at me and says he is pleased with my progress, that I am "becoming." He has never smiled at me before and this is very gratifying to me. They say that I am now ready to meet someone.

We fly together: Altumus on my right, Miraetha on my left, and I am in the middle. We are flying through clouds, a mist. It is beautiful. Straight ahead, the clouds appear as if the sun is shining behind them, trying to break through.

I can see now that behind the clouds is a very bright white-blue light, sort of like the sun, but not exactly. There are light rays—blue-white, white-blue, shimmering crystalline light rays—streaming above, below, and through the clouds. It is just indescribably beautiful.

The clouds begin to part and the light shines through. It is extremely bright, but does not hurt my eyes. I feel myself being drawn toward the light. It emits something so soothing, so comfortable, so assuring. I am filled inside and out with all these feelings of love, joy, peacefulness, and utmost content.

Moving on toward the light, I see that it is a Being—*it is alive, vibrantly alive!* Without a doubt, this is the *most alive* Being I have ever encountered. He is an absolutely radiantly beautiful incredible Being, standing in the midst of the most beautiful, spectacular shimmering shining glowing light that he is emitting. *He is the Light, the Light is him.* As he moves, the light rays radiate his movements. There are no words. No words exist to describe his beauty and person. *Sublime, he is truly sublime.*

I am close enough now to see his face. I recognize him. It is Jesus, the Christ. His *eyes!* Such compassion! He is looking at me. He knows me inside and out! and it's okay. I feel such compassion, acceptance, warmth, kindness, and understanding coming from him. There is a radiation of these feelings from him.

He shows me the Earth, hanging in space. There is something like a halo of shimmering blue, pink, glowing light coming from it. I realize that it is the Earth's aura. The Earth is a living being, too. Looking at it from here I think, "No wonder I chose to come here." The Earth is wonderful, beautiful, and inviting. It beckons to me. I feel such a part of it.

Then he shows me something like a motion picture of the evolution of the Earth. I see that the Earth is progressing, moving, and responding to a universal law.

There is a new stage of evolution, beginning now. The Earth is now entering a stage of attunement, an at-one-ment. And I understand at once why I am here at this time and why I feel what I feel.

So, that was my dream. On awakening, I was so overwhelmed with feelings that I cried. I knew it was more than an ordinary dream, but I didn't know exactly what it was and still don't.

Somehow, in the sleep state, I entered into another dimension of reality. One that was much more real than this one. Christ is alive, he is a living Christ, existing in the present. He is truly present among us and exists with each of us in the "now." Since this dream, I have had a real sense of his presence within me. There still exists that soothing, comfortable, peaceful, presence within me, that I felt in the dream. It is not as intense, but it is definitely still there, and at all times. Sometimes, when I am sad or depressed, I feel it inside of me the most.

I have an understanding now that my personal wants are not as important. They have taken a lower priority. The most important thing is what he wants for me. And so, this is my prayer each and every day, that his will be done through me. And some truly amazing things have happened. It is as if I am being guided by unseen hands in the directions I need to grow spiritually.

I am an ordinary person. I don't know why I had such a special experience. I feel so humbled and unworthy somehow. And yet, the message rings true and clear. I am here for a reason, a purpose. And I must do my part. (2nd P.B.)

P.B.'s confirming, life-transforming experience anchors her sense of life purpose. In her case, she draws meaning from a feeling of partnership with Jesus, from their shared delight in the beauty of life on Earth, from a belief in the meaningfulness of their service to others. The same seems true in the following vision of a 60-year-old woman who had dedicated her life to searching for spiritual truth from the early age of 8.

☞

I laid down the ideal of my life at age 8: Seek ye first the kingdom of God. For many years I have searched and studied the great teachers. So, when at age 60 I had this vision, I understood it as the culmination of all my previous years' efforts.

While meditating, I suddenly became aware of a magnificent steady sound! It was a high-frequency note that reminded me of works by Beethoven and Bach.

I looked up and saw the Lord. He was a brilliant white figure flying from left to right. His arms stretched wide so his garments were his wings. His motion forward made that beautiful sound! On the white garment, every inch of it was covered with human faces. First I was shocked but quickly understood its symbolic meaning: That the whole universe, mankind included, was the body of Christ!

Later, I encountered him again. Again as I sat, a beautiful all-silver androgynous figure appeared. I knew that he was the Lord. Without moving he said:

"I love you till the end of times."

This sentence has become my refuge, my source, and my guide. Such a meeting after sixty years!

I have kept this encounter to myself for many years. You are the second I share it with. (C.M.)

C.M. received the ultimate blessing—a gift of timeless love from the One who is the source of all her strength and the end of all her searching. It would be wonderful if each of us could know, as she did, that this was his gift to us. It's one thing to accept it on faith, and another thing to hear it, to know it.

Jesus bestows this ultimate, timeless gift upon another in the following two Christ encounters. The witness is again M.L.P.—whose other accounts appear in earlier chapters. Here she points out that her earlier experiences were characterized by Jesus appearing to her as all-powerful Master and healer. In the accounts that follow, however, the relationship changes to a more balanced, reciprocal exchange of love and common goals. As the final Christ encounters presented in this book, they reveal a possibility to which a few of the other accounts directly allude—that the Christ encounter provides an opportunity to *love him as he loves us.*

In the dream, I knew that I was on my way to my appointment with him. I was a child, about 9 years old, and I was glad that I had this special meeting with him.

The meeting was on the second floor. The stairs were on the outside of the building. I opened the door, walked a few steps down a hallway, and turned into the room on my right.

He was the only light in the room. It was bare. No other furniture than the straight chair he sat on in the center of the room. He was wearing a white robe.

His smile was warm and welcoming and my heart rushed to him and urged me to follow. I loved him so much. But then I realized that this was something I could give him. That is, if I didn't take up this time with him, it would give him a few minutes to himself.

He sensed this immediately and was grateful for my gift, knowing what a sacrifice it was to leave him.

He smiled, a smile filled with gratefulness.

"As long as I live," he started to say and then stopped, knowing that I would misunderstand. He began again, "Wherever I am, I will always remember you."

I backed out of the room, and when I reached the hall I heard soldiers coming up the stairs.

"They're going to crucify him." I heard my mind scream and I ran screaming down the hall, down the stairs past the soldiers and into consciousness.

This dream was about two years after my first experience. (M.L.P. #3)

The words Jesus spoke to M.L.P. show us again that his commitment to those who love him transcends time and death, and sustains us. M.L.P.'s experience also reveals an astounding possibility: that what *we* do, and how *we* love, somehow sustains him, in return.

Her next two experiences, which took place several years later, also reveal the sense of an evolving partnership.

☞

It was a time in which I was meditating at 2:00 in the morning. However, this experience was in the evening. I was alone in my living room. The evening had a strange quality about it . . . almost a hushedness. Not spooky, but more expectant. Charged, but in a gentle electricity, not the riveting kind. I was standing, doing nothing, when I heard him say: "And in a little while, I'll be with you." Nothing more was said; nothing more was needed. (M.L.P. #4)

☞

The last time I saw Jesus was a face-to-face encounter. I remember only this: I was looking him straight in the eye, person to person. I heard a strength in my voice as I said, almost demanded, not so much asking as requiring: "If I do this, will you be there?"

That was several years ago. I don't know what I agreed to do but I know that he pledged to be there. (M.L.P.#5)

As we review M.L.P.'s Christ encounters, we find that Jesus first comes to her bedside and kneels to pray with her (chapter 2). Soon after, a Being of pure Light heals her physical pain and takes her out of her body to be with him (chapter 3). Then, in the first account in this chapter (M.L.P.#3) she rises from the position of mere supplicant to that of being able to give back the love that has been given to her. And then, her final two accounts (M.L.P.#4, M.L.P.#5) point to the pursuit of mutual goals and an eventual reunion with him.

M.L.P.'s experience suggests that our relationship with Jesus or our own deeper spiritual natures can evolve over time—from an initial act of commitment that may or may not coincide with an actual encounter—to an equal partnership with an exalted being who mirrors back to us what we, ourselves, are becoming. This potential sequence depicts our own destiny as, in essence, very much his own. It presents, at once, an *exalted view* of our importance in the larger scheme of things as well as a *humbling vision* of the awesome responsibilities that stand between us and the greater Home we seek.

10

A Cloud

of Witnesses

> Wherefore seeing we also are compassed about with
> so great a cloud of witnesses, let us lay aside every
> weight, and the sin which doth so easily beset us, and
> let us run with patience the race that is set before us,
> looking unto Jesus, the author and finisher of our
> faith.
>
> —(HEB. 12:1–2A)

It is encouraging that so many individuals have had experiences that point to Jesus' continuing presence in their lives. Knowing this may give others greater hope so that they will eventually enjoy direct encounters with him. An equally profound possibility that I invite you to consider at this point—that *you have already experienced Jesus' presence through your empathic response to the experiences of others.*

I saw evidence of this almost two years ago. As I was leading my

Friday night therapy group, a man told of a Christ encounter that ushered him out of alcoholism and into a life of sobriety. He had been a member of the group for six months but had never mentioned the experience that had become the turning point of his life.

He had been alone in his apartment when he came to the stark realization that alcohol had controlled his life since he was 12. He said to himself, "No more." He wandered about the apartment considering all that would have to change in his life. He stopped to look out of a window and saw a shimmering image. Then, the clear image of Jesus appeared. As he stared spellbound at the image, he found himself in the backyard of his childhood home, imprisoned in a cage. It was the home where he grew up with a domineering father and an alcoholic mother. As a child, he had been caught between them, seeking futilely to please his judgmental father, and trying desperately to heal his mother with his love.

Suddenly in his vision, the bars of the cage lifted, and he was free. This experience became the first step in his difficult journey toward recovery, and has since served as a beacon during times of confusion and despair.

The group was transfixed by the man's tearful story. One woman in particular, an atheist, was moved to speak. She first acknowledged that she had never had such an encounter. But then she stated that she now had a clear sense of what it would be like to have something so important and so central in her life—an event to which everything would have to answer. She said she finally realized what people mean when they speak of having an Ideal. She has since awakened to her own spirituality and has recently joined the Episcopal church.

The man's story seemed to have a quickening effect on all of us. I, for one, felt drawn into Jesus' presence through his experience. This event demonstrated to me once again that a *Christ encounter gathers new witnesses through its sharing.*

Having read this book, you have indirectly experienced dozens of Christ encounters. And you have probably been deeply touched by some of them in particular. Like the woman in my Friday night group, we become witnesses to Jesus' manifestation through our response to these sacred encounters.

This idea may seem strange, especially if you haven't had a direct Christ encounter of your own. You may wonder how your experience of reading these accounts can be compared to meeting Jesus face-to-face.

Think of it this way. Only a few people actually met Jesus during his brief ministry. And of those who did, still fewer understood him well enough to be responsive to his teachings. Isn't it probably true that his disciples and other true followers—both then and now—are simply those who respond to him with love and commitment? And doesn't it also make sense that he realized that these same followers would tell others about their experiences—thereby expanding his reach into the hearts of men and women everywhere? Indeed, his Presence was, and still is, a powerful expanding influence that—like the fishes and loaves—multiplies upon contact with others.

And so, what does it matter whether this response comes through our own direct encounters or through the experiences of others? When we let go of the need to see him, we may find that we already *know* him through the testimonies of others.

Thus we come together as witnesses. And we meet on a common ground through our common response to the Spirit impelling these experiences.

A CALL TO DISCIPLESHIP?

Each of us might ask, what do these experiences mean to *me*? What am *I* called to do? These are difficult questions. But the evidence provided by the Christ encounters strongly suggests one answer: Jesus manifests to call us into a closer relationship with him or with our own deepest potentials. And he seems to expect for us to strive to remain in *constant* relationship, or communion, with him or our spiritual calling.

What *kind* of ongoing relationship does Jesus want? These accounts coincide with the scriptural record that reveals a Master who, in spite of the imperfections in the disciples he chooses, lifts them into *partnership* with him. It's the same spirit of partnership that called common fishermen to become fishers of men. It's the same spirit that summoned Paul to become Apostle to the Gentiles. It's the same spirit that could overlook the betraying nature of Peter and see in him a secure foundation for his church. It's a spirit that calls us to be no less than disciples, seekers of truth even though we remain seriously afflicted by weaknesses and imperfections.

Even if we could bring ourselves to accept the full measure of this invitation, we might still be left wondering what discipleship means *in our everyday lives*. I can only answer this for myself. To me, it simply means living in such a way that my thoughts and actions are considered against the question, *What would* he *do?* In other words, it means *imitating* him to the best of my ability so I can eventually become as he is.

While this might sound presumptuous, I believe it's *all* that Jesus calls us to do. In support of this, Christian writer and spokesman C. S. Lewis says that the imitation of Jesus "is not one among many jobs a Christian has to do; and it is not a sort of special exercise for the top class. It is the whole of Christianity. Christianity offers nothing else at all."[1]

Non-Christian readers may also find in their own sacred traditions the honored practice of imitating the master. Tibetan writer Sogyal Rinpoche extols the virtues of "guru meditation," where the meditator musters an intense devotion and love for a master in an effort to incorporate the master's qualities into himself.[2] From the Hindu tradition, even the *identification* with the master is considered to be a natural stage in one's unfoldment. During his years as a devotee of Guru Nityananda, Muktananda went through an intense period where he confused his identity with that of his own guru's.[3] So we can see that the imitation of Jesus falls within a universal spiritual tradition based on the idea that in order to *become* what one loves, one must imitate the beloved.

POTENTIAL PITFALLS

Of course, most of us will doubtless slip and fall many times as we attempt to imitate him and become full partners with him, with the Spirit. What are the likely pitfalls? I can think of three obvious ones.

Imposing our own narrow desires. We can become so confident we are serving him that we can inadvertently cease listening for his promptings: We can begin to take matters into our own hands. Judas exemplifies one who did this by trying to force Jesus to reveal himself. Apparently, he thought that if he backed Jesus into a corner, Jesus would come out in a blaze of power and glory. Judas was wrong and saw the disastrous consequences of his arrogance. To those of us who are willing to accept a closer relationship with Jesus—or, are more generally committed to our own spiritual unfoldment—we must resist the temptation to push the process too quickly. We need to be content with allowing our spiritual natures to unfold alongside a patient and intentional effort to cooperate in this unfoldment. In our impatience, we can repeat Judas' mistake by requiring a demonstration before a process has reached fruition.

A dream effectively underscored this flaw in me.

⌒

I was back in the time of Jesus, among his close followers. We had been staying in the countryside for some time and did not understand why Jesus was hesitating to go into Jerusalem. We all believed that his entrance into Jerusalem would be the momentous event we had awaited for some time. People would finally proclaim him for who he was. We were all very impatient to be going.

Finally, Jesus told us that it was time to go. As I left the building where we had been staying, I looked up and saw Jesus looking at me out of an upstairs window. His face showed love but deep sadness. I waved enthusiastically. He smiled at me without saying anything, like a parent who accepts that his child doesn't understand. Then we all took off hurriedly in the direction of Jerusalem. As I awoke, I realized in shock what I had failed to grasp in the dream—that he was going to his death. (G.S.S.#10)

Waiting on his promptings can be difficult as long as we cling to what *we* believe is important. And whenever we try to impose our priorities without regard to his, we run the risk of crucifying the very spirit we claim to serve. It is a problem that no doubt afflicts many of us from time to time.

My friend, Mark, discovered this sobering tendency in himself.

He had just finished a demanding four-day conference, in which he had been one of the guest speakers. As he lay down to take a nap, he felt like he had really been working diligently and effectively for God during the previous days. As he drifted off to sleep, a dream unfolded before he lost consciousness. His full wakefulness carried over into the "lucid" dream without a break.

He found himself with three other men and immediately recalled that he met with them every day in his dreams. They formed a group who had a teacher.

As their teacher joined them, Mark saw it was Jesus himself. Jesus began his daily instruction, but Mark's thoughts were already jumping ahead to what he knew would be the culmination of the daily lesson. He remembered that at the end of each lesson, Jesus always gave them a "word for the day." This word expressed the essence of what each of them would be challenged to learn during the upcoming day.

Mark felt an extraordinary desire to know that word. It was as if he had had nothing to drink for a whole day, and the upcoming word was like a glass of water. He was sure his companions felt the same way. Consequently, he was not paying careful attention to what Jesus was saying. Instead, Mark was trying to figure out what the word would probably be—as if the new word would logically follow the words they had been assigned before.

Suddenly, he realized that Jesus was coming to that part of the lesson where the word would be given. To his shock and embarrassment, Jesus said, "I'm unable to give the word today because one among you is impatient and unable to let go and trust." He named no one, but Mark knew it was he. Upon awakening, he realized that Jesus had—lovingly and firmly—held up a magnifying glass to his tendency to preempt the Spirit with his own agenda.

Clinging to Experiences.   Another problem that confronts us as modern disciples is the tendency to become more attached to the *experience* of his presence than to the spiritual life to which he calls us. This is especially likely for those who have already experienced him in a direct way. And it gives a contemporary meaning to Jesus' words to Thomas, "Blessed are they that have not seen, and yet have believed." (John 20:29)

Longfellow's poem "A Theologian's Tale: The Legend Beautiful" eloquently describes the problem of becoming attached to spiritual experiences. Further, Longfellow makes an even stronger statement— that Jesus' continuing presence in our lives *depends* on our putting service to others above our enjoyment of his presence.

The poem opens with a monk praying in his cell. Suddenly, a radiant vision of Jesus appears before him. He is overwhelmed with love and ecstasy and is loath to leave his cell and go about his daily duties. Specifically, the poor await him and his brothers for the food they provide each day. The monk finally tears himself away and finds that the day unfolds magically: Each ordinary duty takes on an air of supreme meaning, and the poor people seem particularly blessed by the food provided by the monks. When he hurries back to his cell at the end of the day, hoping that the vision is still there for him, he finds that Jesus has waited for him. Later, when Jesus finally departs, the monk hears him say: "If thou hadst stayed, I must have fled."

It might seem ironic that the experience of his presence can come to be an obstacle to our serving him. But anyone who has experienced a Christ encounter can become attached to the awesome gift of his confirming presence. Then, rather than forging ahead on our own, we can come to feel inadequate if we can't recapture that sense of presence. My own experience again serves as a good example.

For several years in my early to mid-twenties, I enjoyed numerous deep spiritual experiences and Christ encounters. As the years passed, the experiences slowly diminished in frequency. I missed them, and I wondered if I were doing something wrong. Then, I had a revealing dream that helped me to see the purpose operating behind the diminution of my experiences with him.

In the dream, I was again with his followers and friends. It seemed that we all knew that soon he would no longer be with us. We were saying good-bye to him, one by one. I approached him and embraced him, sobbing deeply. As I turned to walk away, I saw a man whom I knew to be Peter. We embraced each other, sharing our sense of imminent loss. I was profoundly saddened, but I was also aware that Jesus had told us that his departure was necessary for us to develop more fully on our own. (G.S.S. #11)

No matter how much we claim to be our own person, the mere presence of our parents—and other persons of authority—can perpetuate our dependency on them. Eventually, we must strike out on our own before we can mature fully. Similarly, the experience of Jesus' abiding presence can, at times, overshadow our own abilities to become spiritually involved in the lives of those around us.

Fear of Surrendering. Finally, I believe there is a third significant impediment to our accepting the mantle of discipleship: our fear of surrendering fully to a deeper calling that may surprise us with its agenda. We think we can keep something back for ourselves. We want to strike a balance in which we are assured of getting what we want. C. S. Lewis compares this attitude to that of an honest man paying his taxes. "He pays them all right, but he does hope that there be enough left over for him to live on." This does not seem to be what Jesus had in mind. The Christian way, Lewis contends, is much harder and much easier. "Christ says, 'Give me all.' "[4]

Something in us doesn't like this idea. We tremble at the thought of turning over our lives.

The other morning as I awoke, I had an experience that is quite rare for me to have. I heard a voice, and it clearly said to me, "Now is the time for me to lay down my cross, and for you to carry it." On reflection, I believe that the cross signifies to me the exquisite burden of surrendering completely to a life of serving the Master.

Further, I believe that my whole life—and perhaps yours, too—comes down to a single question:

Will you?

Jesus can awaken us to a relationship with him. As the great physician, he can heal our bodies and our hearts. As taskmaster, he can confront and initiate us, encouraging us to remove obstacles to a closer relationship with him. As the consummate teacher, he can instruct and guide us into areas of new growth. And as the bridegroom, he can come to reassure us that we are, above all else, *loved*.

Out of this process can come the realization that *he is alive,* that we are called by a living Master to do more than we've ever imagined: to become his partners and to accept the mantle of discipleship; to imitate him and to grow into a likeness of him.

And short of our full arrival, it might mean falling into error. It might mean imposing our own selfish agendas for a season. It might mean walking alone for long periods without the experience of any consoling presence. And it might mean finally facing our fears of surrendering fully to a spiritual life that ushers us beyond our narrow concerns, and releases us to become what we truly can be.

NOTES

FOREWORD

1. In *The Other Side of Silence* (Mahwah, N.J.: Paulist Press, 1976), *Companions on the Inner Way* (New York: Crossroads, 1983), and *Reaching: The Journey to Fulfillment* (San Francisco: HarperCollins, 1989), I describe a variety of religious experiences. I also present a view of reality that integrates this "other world" and "this world" and give suggestions for those who wish to be closer to the religious dimensions of reality. In my book *God, Dreams and Revelation* (Minneapolis: Augsburg Fortress, 1992), I describe the importance of the dream-vision throughout the history of Christianity.

2. *The Hymnal of the Protestant Episcopal Church in the United States of America* (New York: Church Pension Fund, 1943).

3. A.J. Gordon, *How Christ Came to Church: A Spiritual Biography* (New York: Revell, 1895).

4. Henri Nouwen, *Beyond the Mirror* (New York: Crossroad, 1990).

5. A.M. Greeley, *The Sociology of the Paranormal: A Reconnaissance* (Beverly Hills: Sage, 1975).

6. I have described many of my meditative encounters with Christ in the last chapter of *The Other Side of Silence*. I have described this particular experience in *Christo-Psychology* (New York: Crossroad, 1982).

INTRODUCTION

1. R. Fulop-Miller, *The Saints that Moved the World* (New York: Thomas Crowell, 1945).

2. R.M. Bucke, *Cosmic Consciousness: A Study in the Evolution of the Human Mind* (New York: Dutton, 1969).

3. G. Krishna, *The Biological Basis of Religion and Genius* (New York: Harper & Row, 1972).

4. G.S. Sparrow, *Lucid Dreaming* (Virginia Beach: A.R.E. Press, 1976).

5. R. Moody, *Life After Life* (St. Simons Island, Ga.: Mockingbird, 1975).

6. G.C. Ritchie with E. Sherrill, *Return from Tomorrow* (Waco: Chosen, 1978).

7. B.J. Eadie and C. Taylor, *Embraced by the Light* (Placerville, CA: Gold Leaf Press, 1992).

ONE: AN OVERVIEW OF THE CHRIST ENCOUNTER PHENOMENON

1. T.R. Morton, *Knowing Jesus* (Philadelphia: Westminster, 1974).

2. H. Chadwick, *The Early Church* (New York: Dorset, 1986).

3. S. Daily, *Love Can Open Prison Doors* (San Gabriel: Willing, 1938).

4. Supplement to reading 281–13 of *The Edgar Cayce Readings*, vol. 2 (Virginia Beach: A.R.E. Press, 1974).

5. Ritchie and Sherrill, op. cit.

6. W. Griffin, *Clive Staples Lewis: A Dramatic Life* (San Francisco: Harper & Row, 1986).

7. Fulop-Miller, op. cit.

8. H. Fielding, *Tom Jones* (New York: Random House, 1950).

9. M. Kelsey, *God, Dreams and Revelation* (Minneapolis: Augsburg, 1974).

TWO: THE AWAKENING ENCOUNTER

1. R. Evans, *Dialogue with C. G. Jung* (New York: Praeger, 1981).

2. C.G. Jung. Psychological commentary on R. Wilhelm. *The Secret of the Golden Flower: A Chinese Book of Life* (San Diego: Harcourt Brace Jovanovich, 1961).

3. Lama A. Govinda. *Foundations of Tibetan Mysticism* (New York: Weiser, 1971).

4. Fulop-Miller, op. cit.

THREE: PHYSICAL HEALING AND CONSOLATION

1. Eadie, op. cit.

2. C. Williams, *He Came Down From Heaven* and *Forgiveness of Sins* (London: Faber and Faber, 1950).

3. H. Carpenter, *The Inklings* (London: George Allen and Unwin, 1978).

4. L. Govinda, op. cit.

5. Da Love-Ananda, "The Heart Breaking Truth." Lecture delivered to his followers.

FOUR: EMOTIONAL HEALING

1. C.R. Roger, *On Becoming a Person* (Boston: Houghton Mifflin, 1961).

2. M.S. Peck, *The Road Less Traveled* (New York: Simon & Schuster, 1978).

3. E. Underhill, *Mysticism* (New York: New American Library, 1974).

FIVE: CONFRONTATION: THE BEGINNING OF INITIATION

1. W.Y. Evans-Wentz, ed. *Tibet's Great Yogi Milarepa: A Biography from the Tibetan, by Ras-chun* (London: Oxford University Press, 1928).

2. R. Johnson, *The Fisher King and the Handless Maiden* (San Francisco: Harper San Francisco, 1993).

3. R. Johnson, ibid., p. 24.

4. W.Y. Evans-Wentz, *Tibetan Yoga and Secret Doctrines* (London: Oxford, 1958).

5. D. Brinkley, *Is There Life After Death?* vol. 2 (Dallas: Eclectic Viewpoint, 1993).

SIX: THE CULMINATION OF INITIATION

1. T. Moore, *Care of the Soul* (New York: Walker, 1992).

2. W.Y. Evans-Wentz, op. cit.

3. R. Johnson, *He: Understanding Masculine Psychology* (King of Prussia, PA: Religious Publishing, 1974).

4. C.S. Lewis, *Letters to Malcolm: Chiefly on Prayer* (New York: Harcourt Brace Jovanovich, 1964).

EIGHT: SPIRITUAL INSTRUCTION

1. Ken Wilber, *Up from Eden: A Transpersonal View of Evolution* (Boulder, CO: Shambhala, 1981).

2. M. Kelsey, *Resurrection: Release from Oppression* (Mahwah: Paulist Press, 1985).

3. Eadie, op. cit.

NINE: CONFIRMATIONAL EXPERIENCES

1. St. Teresa, *The Interior Castle*, ed. and trans. E. Allison Peers (Garden City: Doubleday, 1961).

2. W. Starcke, personal communication.

TEN: A CLOUD OF WITNESSES

1. C. S. Lewis, *Mere Christianity* (New York: Macmillan, 1952).

2. S. Rinpoche, *The Tibetan Book of Living and Dying* (San Francisco: Harper San Francisco, 1992).

3. Swami Muktananda, *Play of Consciousness* (San Francisco: Harper & Row, 1978).

4. C.S. Lewis, *Mere Christianity* (New York: Macmillan, 1952).

ACKNOWLEDGMENTS

I want to thank Mark Thurston, who helped me conceive of this project and who has been a great friend on the Path; the members of the Austin study group; Herbert Puryear, whose commitment to Christ and to the understanding of essential Eastern teachings has challenged me to go more deeply into my spiritual practice; Morton Kelsey, Marilyn Peterson, Carol Newell, Michael Reidy, Beth Stevens, Rob Grant, and Cheryl H.—whose belief in this project has helped sustain my own; and to Lynn, for the enriching dialogue we have maintained over the years regarding the Master we have both served.

ABOUT THE AUTHOR

Gregory Scott Sparrow, 43, is a psychotherapist in private practice in Virginia Beach, Virginia. He received his bachelor's degree in psychology from the University of Texas, his master's degree in psychology from West Georgia College, and his doctorate in counseling from the College of William and Mary. His master's thesis and doctoral dissertation focused on the phenomenon of "lucid dreaming," or the experience of becoming aware that one is dreaming during the dream. In 1976, he wrote *Lucid Dreaming—Dawning of the Clear Light*. Widely quoted, it has been hailed as an early classic in this rapidly developing field. He currently specializes in transpersonal approaches to therapy, which include hypnotherapy and an innovative approach to dream work based on his lucid dream research and on ancient principles of Tibetan yoga. He has also authored several articles and home-study courses in the general field of dream theory and dream analysis.

For the past seven years, Dr. Sparrow has been a charter faculty member of Atlantic University in Virginia Beach, which grants a master's degree in transpersonal studies. There he teaches such courses as the Origins and Destiny of Human Consciousness and the Yoga of Dreaming: Advanced Dream Work Methods.

Dr. Sparrow has lectured and taught courses across the U.S. and Canada on meditation, mystical experiences, and dream work methods. He is a student of Jungian psychology, Tibetan Buddhism, and mystical Christianity. For the past four years, he has made a special study of the Christ encounter, which is the visionary or dream experience of meeting Christ face-to-face, on which this book is based. He is also researching encounters with Mary.